LIVERPOOL

PARIS

AUSTRIA-
HUNGARY

ROMANIA

SERBIA

ITALY

LISBON

ALMERÍA

NAPLES

DOCUMENTED
ROUTE

ASSUMED
ROUTE

N

W E

S

An
Adventure in
1914

The True Story of an American Family's

Journey on the Brink of WWI

T. Tileston Wells

Edited by Christopher Kelly

History Invasions Press
1455 NW Leary Way • Suite 400
Seattle • WA • 98107
Phone • 206 489 5335
www.AnAdventureIn1914.com

10 9 8 7 6 5 4 3 2 1

Printed in the United States of America

ISBN 978-0-692-76789-4

Kelly, Christopher (Christopher Robert), 1959 -
Wells, Thomas (Thomas Tileston), 1865 - 1946

An Adventure in 1914 / Christopher Kelly -- Seattle WA : History Invasions Press, [2016]

pages ; cm.

ISBN 978-0-692-76789-4 (hardback)

Summary: *In the summer of 1914, Thomas Tileston Wells, a New York lawyer, traveled through Europe with his wife and two children. But what began as an idyllic summer vacation descended into a nightmare as Europe's armies began mobilizing for the devastating First World War.*

Editor: *Elizabeth Barrett*
Cover Designer: *Blaine Donnelson*
Book Design and Production: *Travis Baechler*
Management: *Vincent Driano*

Dedicated to all the descendants
of Thomas Tileston Wells,
especially Oona, Isabella, and Marco Kelly.

Table of Contents

Illustrations

Maps

Lido Palace Hotel, Italy

Foreword

By Stuart Laycock

It is now over a hundred years since the start of the Great War, a war that ripped Europe apart and, through the mass destruction of mechanized warfare, destroyed many of the certainties of the nineteenth century.

We have all become so used to the grainy black and white photos and the films of both life and large-scale death in the trenches that sometimes it can be hard to find the human angle anymore, to find the link between events of huge political and military significance and human reactions and experiences of the type we can fully understand.

Of all the elements of the First World War, few are more poignant and fascinating than the months and weeks that led to its outbreak, those tense times when peace was still possible, when Europe teetered on the brink and the world held its breath.

From that time comes a fascinating, personal American

account that, in contrast to many more formal accounts, is intensely human both in scale and outlook. This is the story of a tourist and his family, who have set off on holiday, only to find themselves caught up in a global drama. It is the sort of thing that has happened to many American tourists in the century since these events, and it is the sort of thing that could happen to many in the future.

The result is a touching piece of writing that moves from things most have experienced — sightseeing, hiking hills, swimming in lakes — to things that few have — being arrested on suspicion of spying, witnessing the war machine gearing up and beginning to swing into action, both on land and on sea.

T. Tileston Wells, an attorney from New York City, was, of course, not the only American tourist caught up in these events. Another American, James M. Beck (later Solicitor General of the United States), also left behind a brief account of his experiences. In some of his journeys, he retraced the steps of T. Tileston Wells but in the opposite direction, and it is worth reading a portion of Beck's account before moving onto that of Wells:

> On the evening of July 31, 1914, the author reached Basel. The rapid progress of events, narrated in this volume, suggested the wisdom of continuing the journey to Paris that night, but as I wanted to see the tomb of Erasmus in the Basel Cathedral I determined to break my long journey from St. Moritz.

It seemed a fitting time to make a pilgrimage to the last resting-place of the great humanist philosopher of Rotterdam and Louvain, for in that prodigious upheaval of the sixteenth century, which has passed into history as the Reformation, Erasmus was the one noble spirit who looked with a tolerant and philosophical mind upon both parties to the great controversy. He suffered the fate of the conservative in a radical time, and as the great storm convulsed Europe the author of the Praise of Folly probably said on more than one occasion: "A plague o' both your houses." Nearly four centuries have passed since he joined the "silent majority," between whom is no quarreling, and the desolated Louvain, which he loved, is to-day in its ruins a standing witness that immeasurable folly still rules the darkened counsels of men.

As I reached Basel and saw the spires of the Cathedral rising above the Rhine, it seemed to me that the great convulsion, which was then rocking all Europe with seismic violence, was the greatest since that of the French Revolution and might have as lasting results as the great schism of the sixteenth century.

I was not fated to see the tomb, for when I reached my hotel the facilities of civilization had broken down so abruptly that if I did not wish to be interned in Switzerland I must leave early on the following morning for Paris. Transportation had almost entirely collapsed, communication was difficult, and credit itself was so strained that "mine host" of the Three Kings was disposed to look askance even at gold.

Our journey took us to France by way of Delle. Twenty-four hours after we passed that frontier town, German soldiers entered and blew out the brains of a French custom-house officer, thus the first victim in the greatest war that the world has ever known.

As we journeyed from Basel to Paris on that last day of July the fair fields of France never looked more beautiful. In the gleaming summer sun they made a new "field of the cloth of gold," and the hayricks looked like the aureate tents of a mighty army. It was harvest time, but already the laborers had deserted their fields which, although "white unto the harvest," seemed bereft of the tillers. Some had left the bounty of nature to join in the harvest of death. From the high pasture lands of the Alps the herdsmen at the ringing of the village church bells had left their herds and before night had fallen were on their way to the front.

At Belfort the station was crowded with French troops and an elderly French couple came into our compartment. The eyes of the wife were red with weeping, while the man sank into his seat and with his head upon his breast gazed moodily into vacancy. They had just parted with their son, who had joined the colors. I stood for a time with this French gentleman in the corridor of the train, but as he could not speak English or German and I could not speak French, it was impossible for us to communicate the intense and tragical thoughts that were passing through our minds. Suddenly he pointed to the smiling harvest fields, by which we passed so swiftly, and said "Perdu! perdu!" This word of tragical import could have been applied to all civilization as well.

The night of our arrival in Paris I fully expected to see a half a million Frenchmen parading the streets and enthusiastically cheering for war and crying, as in 1870, "à Berlin!" I was to witness an extraordinary transformation of a great nation. An unusual silence brooded over the city. A few hundred people paraded the chief avenues, crying "down with war!", while a separate crowd of equal size sang the national hymn. With these exceptions there was no cheering or enthusiasm, such as I would have expected from my preconceived idea of French excitability. Men spoke in undertones, with a quiet but subdued intensity of feeling rather than with frenzied enthusiasm.[1]

Both Beck and Wells were deeply affected by their experiences in 1914. Both were repelled by the brutality of the Central Powers and the horror of the war. Beck wrote a book, *The War and Humanity* (published in 1916), that criticized the Wilson administration for remaining neutral during the war. Wells wrote *An Adventure in 1914* (never published, but perhaps used as a speech) and threw himself into humanitarian relief work in the Balkans.

---

[1]   James Beck, *The Evidence in the Case* (New York: G. P. Putnam's Sons, 1914).

1ére Classe

Introduction

By Christopher Kelly

The world can change fundamentally in a single day. It has done so many times. The world changed on September 11, 2001; it changed on December 7, 1941. Earlier in the twentieth century, the world was shaken to its foundations on June 28, 1914, with the assassination of Archduke Franz Ferdinand at Sarajevo. Of course, it took longer than one day for World War I to erupt—it took a summer. My great-grandfather, Thomas Tileston Wells, was an eyewitness to that refulgent and transformative summer. An Adventure in 1914 is his testament.

June 28, 1914, marks a sharp dividing line between nineteenth-century ways of thought and the onset of our bleaker modern world. In the space of a few short weeks, the world descended into the maelstrom of the most devastating war in human history up to that point. Mighty empires would be toppled, revolution would radically transform Russia, and millions would be killed. The glory of the Belle Époque would be erased by trench warfare on the Western Front. In the summer of 1914, the waltz ended and a long muddy slog began.

Prior to that time, Europe seemed blessed by peace, prosperity, and technical advancement. Industrialization created vast economic gains that filtered to most levels of society. Scientific and medical progress dramatically increased life spans in the Western world. The introduction of canning improved food safety. Railways and steamships made travel easier than ever before. Hotels and restaurants flourished, catering to the tourist trade. In August of 1908, the Wright brothers publicly demonstrated human-controlled flight in France before Britain's King Edward VII and other luminaries. Later that year, in Le Mans, Wilbur Wright declared, "Princes & millionaires are thick as fleas."

The increased ease of travel and communication meant that the world was more cosmopolitan and better informed than ever before. Russia was closely connected to Europe, with most of its aristocracy still speaking French, as it had for two hundred years. Englishmen read Russian novels. Newspapers in cities around the world gained in circulation, and newspaper owners like William Randolph Hearst became princely power brokers. In 1901, an Italian, Guglielmo Marconi, transmitted radio messages across the Atlantic, sparking an electronic media revolution.

The world was not merely making progress and evolving. It was celebrating its newly created wealth with extravagant festivals and exhibitions. The modern Olympic movement encouraged peaceful competition between nations when it was kicked off in Athens in 1896. The Paris Exposition of 1900 featured exhibitions by over forty countries and proclaimed itself a "symbol of harmony and peace" for all humanity. Electric lighting was replacing the gaslights of the Victorian era, which had the benefit of making European streets safer.

But the lights were about to go out all over Europe.[1]

The assassinations of June 1914 would be succeeded by the ultimatums and mobilizations of July, and would ultimately lead to the guns of August.

The world began its march to war on June 28, 1914, when Franz Ferdinand, the Austrian archduke and heir to the throne, paid a visit to Sarajevo. His wife Sophie was excited to be accompanying him on their wedding anniversary. A band of no less than six assassins, affiliated with a Serbian nationalist secret society called the Black Hand, awaited him. A bomb was hurled near the archduke's Gräf & Stift convertible, wounding an Austrian officer. The archduke insisted on giving his planned speech at the Sarajevo Town Hall before proceeding to the hospital. Gavrilo Princip, a nineteen-year-old Bosnian Serb, spotted their motorcade and fired his revolver twice. The archduke was heard to mutter, "Sophie, Sophie, don't die, stay alive for our children," but both were dead within minutes. The peace of Europe was extinguished soon after.

---

1   "The lamps are going out all over Europe, we shall not see them lit again in our life-time." Sir Edward Grey, British foreign secretary, 1905–1916

Basel Cathedral, Switzerland

For nearly a century after Napoleon's defeat at Waterloo on June 18, 1815, another day that changed the world, a general peace had prevailed in Europe. At the conclusion of that battle, the Duke of Wellington shook hands with the Prussian general Blücher at an inn aptly named La Belle Alliance—the beautiful alliance. A huge painting celebrating this moment can still be found in the British Houses of Parliament.

By 1914, however, the Anglo-Prussian alliance was a distant memory. Europe was an armed camp perched on a precipice. Austria-Hungary was allied with Germany as the Central Powers. France, aggrieved at having lost Alsace and Lorraine in the Franco-Prussian War, was allied with Russia and the British Empire. Italy was loosely allied to the Central Powers, but was also sympathetic to Serbian aspirations and highly skeptical of Austrian intentions. The Anglo-German relationship had been frayed to the breaking point by a costly naval arms race. Which power could build dreadnoughts fastest to maintain its imperial possessions around the world?

Millions of men stood ready to mobilize across the Continent. Officers on both sides anxiously consulted their railway timetables, convinced that whichever side mobilized first was destined to prevail in any conflict. This theory ran aground when Czarist Russia, the first to mobilize, was decisively defeated in the war.

The alliance system that divided Europe into opposed camps was the war's powder keg. Tension in the Balkans was the match that lit the fuse, and our world was engulfed in the ensuing explosion.

La Musée de l'Armée, Paris

Friedrich Nietzsche, a philosophical Cassandra, had predicted it. In 1888, he wrote, "There will be wars the like of which have never been seen on earth before."

Technological progress had helped create wealth. But some realized that the resulting new age of industrial warfare, with machine guns, military aviation, and poison gas, would lead to a war more destructive than all the wars that had preceded it.

Others who sensed the coming danger opposed all war on philosophical grounds. In 1912, hundreds of delegates from socialist parties all over Europe met in the Swiss city of Basel to protest the outbreak of the first Balkan war.

They gathered at Basel's ancient red sandstone cathedral. Jean Jaurès, a French socialist leader destined for assassination in July 1914, asserted, "We will leave this hall committed to the salvation of peace and civilization." Starting in 1904, William Jennings Bryan, the American Secretary of State from 1913–1915, frequently delivered a ringing antiwar speech titled "The Prince of Peace." In 1909, President William Howard Taft gave a speech in which he urged that "war should be abolished."

Thomas Tileston Wells

Thomas Tileston Wells, my maternal great-grandfather and the author of *An Adventure in 1914*, grew up in a burgeoning country. When he was born at 2 East Fourteenth Street in New York City (now the site of a New School campus) on September 12, 1865, there were only thirty-five states in the Union. Nevada would be added later that year. By the time he wrote *An Adventure in 1914*, the country had grown to forty-six states. From 1870 to 1910, the US population more than doubled, from 38.1 million to 92.2 million. High birth rates and a flood of immigrants, many from southern and eastern Europe, fueled this explosive population growth.

The US economy more than quintupled in terms of GDP from 1870 to 1913. US manufacturing surpassed that of the British Empire for the first time in 1895. Personal incomes were on the rise.

In the 1912 presidential election, President Taft, the incumbent, was challenged by Teddy Roosevelt, who ran in the newly created Progressive Party, aka the Bull Moose Party, producing a fissure in the Republican Party. The result of that fall's three-way race was the election of Woodrow Wilson, a progressive Democrat and the former president of Princeton University.

Politicians did not fail to notice the nation's growing incomes. In 1913, the Sixteenth Amendment to the

Constitution was ratified by the states, creating a peacetime income tax for the first time in US history. That same year, the Federal Reserve was established.

Americans were hard at work expanding the nation's economy. They were inventing new technologies and taking out patents. The Wright Brothers were the first to succeed at pilot-controlled, motor-powered flight at Kitty Hawk, North Carolina, in 1903. Americans could read all about their nation's dynamic progress in newspapers produced by William Randolph Hearst and others.

America's new wealth also led to an increase in leisure activities. Baseball was the national pastime. In 1914, Ty Cobb led the American League with a .368 batting average, and the Boston Braves swept the World Series in four games. On October 9, 1915, Woodrow Wilson became the first sitting president to attend a World Series and throw out the first pitch, when the newly christened Boston Red Sox defeated the Phillies at the Baker Bowl in Philadelphia by a score of two to one. The Red Sox would go on to win the pennant that year, taking it in four games to one.

There was an explosion in tourism and travel technology as well. The first model T rolled off Henry Ford's assembly lines in 1908. Railroads crisscrossed the continent, making long-distance travel easy and affordable. In spite of the sinking of the *Titanic* in 1912, the golden age of the ocean liner was in full swing. The cost of a first-class transatlantic ticket on the Cunard line was 30 guineas, which would be the equivalent of $3,000 to $4,000 today.

Portrait of Grace Wells (née Tileston), mother of Thomas Tileston Wells

St. Mark's School Southborough, Massachusetts ca. 1880

Many Americans in 1914 were inward looking, concerned mainly with living their private lives. "Why should we be concerned about squabbles in Europe between countries that many Americans could not even find on a map?" they asked. Hadn't George Washington counseled against "foreign entanglements" in his farewell address?

But Thomas Tileston Wells, the son of John and Grace

Wells, was a member of a privileged class. His father was a New York lawyer. T. T. Wells was descended from an old colonial New York family. An ancestor, Robert Wells, was killed by Native Americans in the Cherry Valley Massacre in 1778 during the American Revolution. In 1878, T. T. Wells was enrolled as a first former (seventh grade) at St. Mark's School in Southborough, Massachusetts. His best subjects were history, French, physics, botany, and composition. Wells also played tennis at St. Mark's. In the fall of 1882, the entire school was awoken in the middle of the night to observe the Great Comet of 1882 that blazed "like a scimitar in the eastern sky."

In 1883, Wells withdrew from St. Mark's to spend his senior year at the elite Institut Le Rosey in Rolle, Switzerland, which had been founded in 1880 by Paul-Émile Carnal. It was at Le Rosey, situated by Lake Geneva, that he may have developed the love of nature that is on display throughout *An Adventure in 1914*. His time at Le Rosey also developed a keen, lifelong interest in the world beyond American shores. Today, Le Rosey is known as the most expensive high school in the world. Annual tuition clocks in at over $133,000 per year. The sons and daughters of billionaires and royalty attend this elite school, which moves to its winter campus in Gstaad, Switzerland, during the ski season.

Wells's life was bookended by conflict. He was born in 1865, the final year of the US Civil War—the bloodiest war in American history. He died in 1946, just after the close of World War II—the bloodiest war in human history. But Wells was not a soldier.

Columbia Law School, New York

After high school, Wells returned to New York and attended Columbia College, but he did not graduate. He passed an examination by the Board of Regents of the University of the State of New York and was accepted into a two-year program at The School of Law at Columbia College (now Columbia Law School). Columbia Law already enjoyed a distinguished reputation in legal circles. Francis Lieber (1798–1872), a Prussian who was wounded in the Waterloo campaign, immigrated to America and became a law professor at Columbia. Lieber wrote the code of conduct for the Union Army in the US Civil War, which became the foundation for the Geneva Conventions that followed. Wells attended lectures at the law school on East Forty-Ninth Street and earned a degree in 1888.

Wells was a lawyer with the New York City firm of Lexow, MacKellar & Wells from 1898 to 1916, but his interest in Europe remained. He was a regular passenger on transatlantic ocean liners for much of his long life. In the spring of 1909, for example, he took the RMS *Lusitania* from New York to Liverpool. This Cunard ship would be sunk by a torpedo launched by a German U-boat in World War I, killing around 1,200 passengers on May 7, 1915.

Wells was a lifelong Francophile who became the honorary president of the French Alliance in New York City. In 1910, Wells was decorated with the French *Légion d'Honneur*—the highest civilian and military decoration in France.

In 1918, Wells became the Romanian consul general to America, based in New York City. He served for ten years as consul general, and continued to serve as honorary consul general until 1941.

Almost every summer for many years, Wells sailed from New York to Europe, and then traveled on to Bucharest by train. He often traveled with his family, as he did in 1914. He came to know the Romanian royal family quite well.

Wells had a reputation for being a bit of a ladies' man. He was even rumored to have had an affair with Queen Marie of Romania.[2] The queen and her husband, King Ferdinand, had what would today be called an "open" marriage. Queen Marie was rumored to have had numerous affairs, including with at least one other American, Waldorf Astor.

In my earlier work, *America Invades*, my coauthor and I wrote:

> Queen Marie [was] a granddaughter of Queen Victoria and daughter of Prince Alfred, brother of the future King Edward VII. During World War I, Romania, like us, initially remained neutral, but later, influenced by Queen Marie, joined the Allied side. As a result, most of Romania ended up being occupied by enemy troops in the ensuing conflict.

---

2   This is based on interviews with Mrs. Howard Townsend, whose source was Wells's daughter, Mrs. Georgina Van Rensselaer..

Queen Marie of Romania

Train, Buchs, Switzerland

However, Queen Marie, with the assistance of her friend, the American dance pioneer Loie Fuller, got hold of a major American loan that helped the Romanians to resist.

When the Russian Revolution took Russia out of the war, Romania found it could not fight on alone, and it was forced to seek peace with the enemy. It only reentered the war (on the Allied side) on November 10, 1918, a day before the armistice.

In 1919, after the Allied victory, Romania received some compensation for all its suffering. Thanks largely, once again, to the energetic efforts of Queen Marie, Romania acquired large tracts of territory that had previously been part of the Austro-Hungarian and Russian Empires.

In 1914, Wells was a forty-nine-year-old New York lawyer. He was relatively tall at five foot eleven, with blue eyes. He wore a mustache, and his brown hair was tinged with gray. His wife was Georgina Betts, and they had an eighteen-year-old son, John, and eleven-year-old daughter, Georgina. Their younger son Rossiter had died tragically of whooping cough at age two in 1902.

Wells could be a stubborn man. In a 1924 letter written by his wife on board an eastbound Orient Express in Transylvania, she groused, "We are disappointed, Georgina and I that TTW [Thomas Tileston Wells] wont [sic] stop over at Budapest, but he simply wont, and we are grateful to get two days at Vienna."

Café Liégeois

Wells and his family embarked from America on a transatlantic liner bound for Europe on June 24, 1914. They would have been approaching the coast of Europe when Archduke Ferdinand was assassinated on June 28. Wells and his family almost certainly traveled by train to Paris. Supremely confident of their travel plans, they came laden with many steamer trunks but no passports. (The widespread use of passports came as a direct result of World War I.) Wells was, however, carrying a letter of introduction written by Secretary of State William Jennings Bryan. This proved fortuitous.

In a Paris brasserie, eleven-year-old Georgina might have enjoyed a café viennois dessert made with coffee, ice cream, and whipped cream. In just a few weeks' time, the sweet concoction would be renamed a café liégeois to honor the Belgians' stout defense of their city, Liège, from the German invaders. The summer of 1914 would transform our world in ways large and small.

Chronology

Thomas Tileston Wells

September 12, 1865	Thomas Tileston Wells born to John Wells and Grace Tileston Wells in New York City, New York
Fall 1878	Wells enrolls St. Mark's School, Southborough, Massachusetts
Fall 1883	Wells attends Institut Le Rosey, Switzerland
Fall 1884	Wells enrolls Columbia College
Fall 1886	Wells enrolls the School of Law at Columbia College
1888	Wells graduates the School of Law at Columbia College
1890	Wells admitted to the New York bar
1896–1916	Wells works as lawyer at Lexow, MacKellar & Wells
May 10, 1895	Birth of son John Wells
October 5, 1902	Birth of daughter Georgina Lawrence Wells
1908	Austria-Hungary annexes Bosnia
May 25, 1909	Wells arrives in Liverpool on board the *Lusitania*
1910	Wells awarded the *Légion d'Honneur*
1912	Wells awarded doctor of letters, Rutgers University
June 20, 1914	Secretary of State William Jennings Bryan signs letter for Wells
June 24, 1914	Wells and family leave United States for Europe
June 28, 1914	Archduke Franz Ferdinand and wife Sophie assassinated in Sarajevo, Bosnia

July 13, 1914	Wells and family depart Paris by train, headed to Mulhouse, France
July 14 –22, 1914	Wells and family visit Basel, Zurich, Liechtenstein, and Innsbruck
July 23, 1914	Wells and family return to Innsbruck
July 23, 1914	Austria-Hungary sends ultimatum to Serbia
July 28, 1914	Austria-Hungary declares war on Serbia
July 30, 1914	Wells and family leave Cortina
July 31, 1914	Wells and family arrive Bolzano (Bozen)
August 1, 1914	Wells and family visit Trent
August 1, 1914	Wells and family arrive at Riva on Lake Garda
August 1, 1914	Germany and Russia declare war on each other, France mobilizes
August 1, 1914	Italy declares its neutrality
August 2, 1914	Wells arrested by Austrian authorities, leaves Riva for Italy
August 2, 1914	Germany invades Luxembourg
August 3, 1914	Germany declares war on France
August 4, 1914	Germany invades Belgium, Britain declares war on Germany, USA announces neutrality
August 4–16, 1914	Siege of Liège, Belgium
August 5, 1914	Wells applies for US passport in Venice, Italy
August 7, 1914	British Expeditionary Force begins to arrive in France
August 7–10, 1914	Battle of Mulhouse
August 20, 1914	Pius X dies in Rome
August 23–30, 1914	Russians defeated at Battle of Tannenberg
September 2, 1914	Wells and family at St. Peter's, Rome

September 3, 1914	Benedict XV chosen as new Pope
September 5–12, 1914	First Battle of the Marne
September 10, 1914	Wells and family leave Naples on board SS *Canopic* with three cardinals
September 13, 1914	SS *Canopic* arrives Almería, Spain
September 17, 1914	SS *Canopic* arrives Azores
September 24, 1914	SS *Canopic* arrives Boston, Massachusetts
May 7, 1915	*Lusitania* sunk by German U-boat
May 23, 1915	Kingdom of Italy declares war on Austria-Hungary
1915–1918	Wells serves as chairman of Serbian Relief Committee of America (aka Serbian Relief)
April 4, 1917	US Senate votes to declare war on Germany
February 1918	Wells begins serving the Kingdom of Romania as temporary consul in New York
November 11, 1918	World War I ends
April 26, 1919	Wells is appointed by the decree of King Ferdinand I as honorary consul of Romania in New York
1926	Wells coordinates the visit of Queen Marie of Romania to the United States
March 30, 1928	Birth of Wells's granddaughter Nina Van Rensselaer
March 31, 1932	Birth of Wells's granddaughter Catherine Van Rensselaer
July 18, 1938	Death of Queen Marie of Romania
December 12, 1941	Romania declares war on the United States
1941	Wells resigns as honorary consul of Romania
April 30, 1945	Colonel William Darby killed in Torbole, Italy
April 23, 1946	Thomas Tileston Wells dies in New York, age 80

Franco-Prussian War statue, Belfort, France

Franco-Prussian War Prelude

It has become commonplace for historians to discuss the ways in which World War I and the harsh peace terms imposed in the Treaty of Versailles "caused" World War II. Less well understood is the manner in which the Franco-Prussian War laid the groundwork for the First World War.

Sheep are, in general, white, but that does not preclude the existence of black sheep. In the time from Napoleon's defeat at Waterloo on June 18, 1815, until August of 1914, Europe was, in general, at peace. That did not preclude occasional wars, however. These included the Crimean War (1853–56), the Austro-Prussian War (1866), and the Franco-Prussian War (1870–71).

The Franco-Prussian War destroyed forever the pretensions of Napoleon III's Empire. The war lasted just over nine months, from July 19, 1870–May 10, 1871. At the Battle of Sedan on September 1, 1870, French forces were routed by the Germans, armed with needle guns, who marched under the banner of Gott mit uns (God with us). Paris was surrounded by German troops and besieged. Parisians

Napoleon III, French Foreign Legion Museum, Aubagne, France

were forced to eat dogs and rats. In the spring of 1871, the revolutionary Paris Commune flared up for a couple of months in the besieged capital.

Napoleon III fled with his family to exile in London, where he threw himself onto the mercy of his wine merchant. Today one can find the Napoleon Cellar at Berry Brothers & Rudd on St. James Street. This is a fitting monument to the man who first requested the Bordeaux Classification of 1855 for the Exposition Universelle in Paris.

The French defense of Belfort in the Vosges Mountains was the heroic exception to France's dismal performance during the Franco-Prussian War. Pierre Philippe Denfert-Rochereau, the commander of Belfort, held out for over a hundred days against much larger Prussian forces. He became known as the Lion of Belfort, and is commemorated notably with the statue of an immense sandstone lion. The sculptor of this monument, Frédéric Auguste Bartholdi, also designed New York's Statue of Liberty.

At the end of the war, France was dismembered, losing the provinces of Alsace and Lorraine, which were annexed by Imperial Germany. In 1894, the French Republic, the most liberal government in Europe, allied itself with Czarist Russia, the most autocratic government in Europe, partially in order to regain its lost provinces. When Alsace and Lorraine had been annexed by Germany, a black shroud was used to cover a Parisian statue that represented Strasbourg, the capital of Alsace. In August of 1914, as war clouds gathered across Europe, a vast crowd assembled around the shrouded statue and stripped it of its mourning crepe. The birthplace of Raymond Poincaré, the fiercely anti-German president of the French Republic at the outbreak of World War I, was Bar-le-Duc — a town in Lorraine that had been occupied by German troops for three years.

Many Germans drew the conclusion from the Franco-Prussian War that military adventurism could swiftly result in decisive and glorious victory. William I, the Prussian king, was crowned emperor of Germany in 1871 in Louis XIV's Hall of Mirrors at Versailles. This was also the war that forged Bismarck's unified Germany, and it was just the type of war that Kaiser William II hoped would advance the German imperial project in the summer of 1914. The philosopher Friedrich Nietzsche, who served as a medical orderly in the Franco-Prussian War, declared, "You say it is the good cause that justifies even war? I say to you: it is the good war which justifies every cause." Many German soldiers would mobilize in the summer of 1914 with copies of Nietzsche's *Thus Spake Zarathustra*, in their backpacks.

The war that united Germany also had profound consequences for Italy. With the onset of war, France withdrew its garrison from Rome, where it had been protecting Pope Pius IX and the Papal States from being incorporated into a unified Italy, to support France's campaign against the Prussians. The Kingdom of Italy seized this opportunity to

Friedrich Nietzsche

invade the Eternal City and make Rome its new capital. Pope Pius IX's armies were defeated and the Papal States were dissolved. Italy was a united nation, and no pope would ever again send armies into battle.

The Lion of Belfort, France

An Adventure in 1914

By Thomas Tileston Wells

Original Text Manuscript

With Historical Commentary by Christopher Kelly

THE BATTLE
OF MULHOUSE

The town of Mulhouse that Wells visited in July 1914 was a battlefield by August.

According to the Schlieffen Plan, the German Army would swing through Belgium and Luxembourg in any war with France. The French Army also planned offensive moves at the outset of war with Germany. They would attack farther south into Alsace and Lorraine — the provinces that had been lost in the Franco-Prussian War.

The Battle of Mulhouse, fought in Alsace in August 1914, was a direct result of these plans. The French Army had some initial success with its offensive. It managed to capture three thousand German prisoners, and Mulhouse was occupied. General Joffre proclaimed on August 7, 1914:

CHILDREN of ALSACE!
After forty-four years of sorrowful waiting, French soldiers once more tread the soil of your noble country. They are the pioneers in the great work of revenge. For them what emotions it calls forth, and what pride!

To complete the work they have made the sacrifice of their lives. The French nation unanimously urges them on, and in the folds of their flag are inscribed the magic words, "Right and Liberty."

Long live Alsace.

Long live France.

In the face of German counterattacks, however, French forces withdrew from Mulhouse the end of August. The French suffered about four thousand casualties; the Germans, about three thousand. German pressure on the northern side of the front forced the French to abandon offensive activity in Alsace and redeploy their forces to fight the Battle of the Marne.

$\mathcal{W}$ith my wife, son and daughter I left Paris early in the morning of July 13th for a little trip through the Austrian Tyrol and the region of the Dolomites. That afternoon we

Arc de Triomphe, Paris, France

arrived at Belfort near the frontier between French and German Alsace; saw the lion carved in the rock which commemorates the heroic defense of the town in 1870 against the Germans, the heavy forts and many soldiers, but we did not then think that these soldiers and forts would be so soon engaged in deadly contest. We then went on in the train and stopped a few minutes on the French frontier town of Petit Croix. We went on from Petit Croix to Altkirch and Mulhouse, or Muhlhausen, as it is called in Germany, where the terrible battles were fought in the early part of this war, these cities being repeatedly taken and lost by both sides. All these names have since become familiar to us owing to the war.

RENOVATUM ET AMPLI
FICATUM ANNO DOMINI
MDCCCCI

Rathaus, Basel, Switzerland

Swan, Lake Zurich, Switzerland

$\mathcal{F}$rom there we went on to Bâle, or as the Germans call it, Basel, in Switzerland, and on the Rhine. All this country looked peaceful enough when we passed through it, but the German military spirit and their overbearing ways were visible even then. For instance, the Customs House inspector came through the train on the German frontier but refused to speak anything but German and we had to say, "Wir haben nicht zu zollern."[1]

We spent the night at Basel, but had time to see the picturesque old city and the red cathedral and town hall all covered with pictures, and the swift flowing Rhine running through the town, before we left the next day for Zurich.

We spent a couple of days at Zurich. One day we went up the lake in a steamer and took tea at the other end. The country about this lake is not very high, but the lake is very picturesque, and when it is very clear you can get glimpses of the distant snow-covered mountains beyond the hills which immediately border the lake.

---

1   Meaning uncertain. From the context, Wells seems to have meant, "We have nothing to declare," but the German for that would be *"Wir haben nichts zu erklären."*

LIECHTENSTEIN

The Principality of Liechtenstein is a European microstate sandwiched between Switzerland and Austria.

In 1914, Franz I was the prince of Liechtenstein. In spite of his strong Habsburg connections, he kept Liechtenstein neutral in the Great War. Franz I also finished restoring the fairytale castle in Vaduz in 1912, two years prior to the visit of Wells and his family. The old train station in Schaan has been preserved and looks much as it did in 1914.

Today Liechtenstein is renowned for its postage stamps and picturesque mountain scenery. The principality is also noted for its prosperity and peacefulness. Its 37,000 citizens rank among the wealthiest in the world in terms of per capita GDP. Liechtenstein abolished its army in 1868 and remained neutral in both world wars.

Wells, aware that a permanent income tax had just been imposed in the United States in 1913, seems to have been envious of Liechtenstein's lack of income taxes. Today, however, the principality's citizens do pay some taxes.

*W*hen we left Zurich we went right through in the train to Innsbruck in the Tyrol. On our way we passed the picturesque lake of Walensee, surrounded by high mountains, and then crossed the Rhine into the little principality of Liechtenstein; and as the train stopped for a few minutes near the capital, Schaan-Vaduz, we got out to be able to say that we had been in that country. This little state has no taxes as its prince personally pays all the expenses. He has vast estates and generally lives in Vienna.

Vaduz Castle, Principality of Liechtenstein

DID WELLS REALLY MEET
NIKOLA PAŠIĆ IN JULY 1914?

According to Wells's account, he had a "nice chat" with Nikola Pašić in the dining car of a train headed from Switzerland to Innsbruck, Austria, on or around July 16, 1914.

This is really an extraordinary claim. Pašić, the Serbian prime minister, was one of the central characters of the July Crisis of 1914. He did have connections to Switzerland, having earned an engineering degree from the Polytechnic School in Zurich.

The assassination of the Austrian archduke took place in Sarajevo on June 28. Wells tells us that he did not leave Paris until July 13, and that he spent two nights in Zurich.

There was an election going on in Serbia in July 1914. We know that Pašić was campaigning in Nish on July 23, 1914, when the Austrians delivered their ultimatum. At that point, he rushed back to Belgrade.

Would Pašić really have left Serbia during the election and during an existential crisis for his nation? Furthermore, in 1914, Innsbruck was Austrian territory, as it remains to this day. Would Pašić have dared risking arrest by Austrian authorities by journeying outside of Serbia at this time? Only something incredibly important could have drawn him into such a risky undertaking.

Did Wells embellish his account of this meeting with Pašić? Perhaps Wells was confused in identifying the Serbian prime minister? Field Marshall Radomir Putnik, for example, was another bearded Serbian leader who, with the outbreak of war, was definitely allowed to travel from Budapest to Belgrade. On the other hand, Wells does seem to be a credible witness, relaying an understated account of the chance meeting with Pašić.

A perusal of the diplomatic Serbian correspondence for 1914, known as the Serbian Blue Book[1] (from the Ministry of Foreign Affairs of the Republic of Serbia), is instructive. On July 14, Pašić sent a message (#21) from Belgrade to all Serbian legations that, contrary to the reports in Austro-Hungarian newspapers, "complete calm prevails in Belgrade." His next message (#30) was sent from Belgrade on July 19. This lengthy and urgent message speaks directly to the dilemma facing Serbia:

> *The Serbian Government consider that their vital interests require that peace and tranquillity [sic] in the Balkans should be firmly and lastingly established. And for this very reason they fear lest the excited state of public opinion (con't)*

---

[1]   http://www.mfa.gov.rs/en/diplomatic-tradition/historical-diplomatic-papers/1293--1914

*T*hen the train went on into the Austrian territory and we went up the valley of the Ill with towering snow-covered mountains on either side, and finally reached the Arlberg tunnel which brought us into the upper Inn valley; and we went on down that valley until we came to the beautiful old city of Innsbruck.

In the dining car on that train, my son and I happened to sit opposite the great Monsieur Pachitch,[2] the Prime Minister of Serbia, and we had a nice chat with him, but did not mention politics. He was dissatisfied with the service and the lunch and wrote out a complaint, but he gave the waiter a tip of 5 Kronen[3] – an unusually large sum.

Dining car, Cité du Train, Mulhouse, France

Five Kronen, Austria

---

2   "The great Monsieur Pachitch," or Nikola Pašić, was the prime minister of Serbia during the July crisis of 1914.

3   About $1.00 in 1914 or about $25.00 in 2016.

(con't) in Austria-Hungary may induce the Austro-Hungarian Government to make a demarche* which may humiliate the dignity of Serbia as a State, and to put forward demands which could not be accepted.

I have the honour therefore to request you to impress upon the Government to which you are accredited our desire to maintain friendly relations with Austria-Hungary, and to suppress every attempt directed against the peace and public safety of the neighbouring Monarchy. We will likewise meet the wishes of the Austro-Hungarian Empire in the event of our being requested to subject to trial in our independent Courts any accomplices in the outrage who are in Serbia – should such, of course, exist.

But we can never comply with demands which may be directed against the dignity of Serbia, and which would be inacceptable to any country which respects and maintains its independence.

Between July 14 and July 19, there were no outgoing messages from Pašić. It was during this gap in correspondence that Pašić might conceivably have journeyed out of Serbia and encountered Wells on a train.

The Austrian ultimatum of July 23 was precisely the démarche that Pašić feared.

At the end of the day, Wells's account seems to deepen the mystery that swirled around Pašić during the July Crisis.

*démarche: a line of action; move; countermove; maneuver, especially in diplomatic relations

Nikola Pasic, Serbian Prime Minister 1914

NIKOLA PAŠIĆ AND THE AUSTRIAN ULTIMATUM

The July Crisis of 1914 that led to World War I was, perhaps, the greatest train wreck in history. But was it an accident or was it something even more sinister... perhaps even a conspiracy? At the heart of this mystery stands the controversial figure of Nikola Pašić (1845–1926). Did the Serbian prime minister know in advance of the plot to assassinate Archduke Franz Ferdinand in Sarajevo? To this day, historians remain divided on the question of whether he knew; and if he knew, how much he knew and whether or not he tried to stop the plot.

The Austrians certainly accused the Serbian government of complicity in the assassination of the archduke. It is probable that Austrian fears were justified. Pašić may have had an informant, Milan Ciganović, who worked in the Serbian railways and was charged with monitoring the Black Hand, a secret Serbian group that supported the liberation of all Serbs and helped in planning the assassination. It was Ciganović who actually supplied weapons and trained the conspirators who struck the blows against Austria. The Serbian government had Ciganović packed off to the United States for the duration of the war.

On July 23, 1914, the Austrians delivered an ultimatum to the Serbian government. They demanded the immediate arrest of Ciganović, the use of Austrian investigative police inside Serbia, and the suppression of subversive movements.

Pašić was not in Belgrade when this ultimatum was delivered, as he was campaigning for re-election. On July 25, Russia's czar, Nicholas II, reassured his Serbian ally by ordering all final-year cadets to officer rank—a clear sign of mobilization. That same day, Pašić rejected the Austrian ultimatum as unacceptable to Serbian sovereignty and began mobilization of Serbian forces. On the night of July 29, Nicholas II signed the order for general mobilization in support of his Serbian ally.

The day before, on July 28, 1914, Franz Joseph, the eighty-three-year-old emperor of Austria-Hungary, had signed the Austrian declaration of war against Serbia. By 1916, all of Serbia was occupied by Austro-Hungarian forces. Serbia would pay an enormous price; over a million Serbians died in the war out of a population of about four and a half million.

After Allied victory in 1918, Pašić became prime minister of the newly formed Kingdom of Serbs, Croats and Slovenes that was created by the *(con't)*

Statue of Nikola Pašić, Zajecar, Serbia
(Photo courtesy of Milena Mihajlovic)

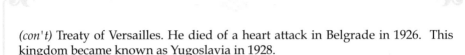

(con't) Treaty of Versailles. He died of a heart attack in Belgrade in 1926. This kingdom became known as Yugoslavia in 1928.

The conclusions of many historical accounts of the July Crisis can be read like the denoument of the parlor game Clue. There are a limited number of suspects who were in a position to either accelerate or slow the march to war by their respective countries. So who killed Mr. Boddy? Who bears the responsibility for starting World War I? Was it Kaiser Wilhelm in the library with a toy battleship? Was it Czar Nicky in the conservatory with a premature mobilization? Some historians even seem to suggest that the July Crisis was more like Agatha Christie's *Murder on the Orient Express*, where all suspects had a hand in the deed.

If we allow ourselves to consider the start of this world war as not merely a catastrophe but an actual crime, then it does not seem inappropriate to ask the classic question posed by detectives: "Cui bono?" Who benefited from the outbreak of World War I? The Russian czar and his family were butchered in Yekaterinburg by the Reds in 1918. Kaiser Wilhelm II was forced to abdicate his throne and go into exile in Holland. Franz Joseph died in 1916, and the Austro-Hungarian Empire was dismantled. The Ottoman Empire was dismembered as well, with consequences for the Middle East rippling down to our own time. France was bled white, and the British Empire lost nearly a million men in combat.

Serbia suffered enormously from the war; and this clearly affected Wells, who became the chairman of the Serbian Relief Committee of America during the war. But that suffering notwithstanding, Nikola Pašić did emerge after the war as the prime minister of an expanded Serbian-led kingdom.

*I*nnsbruck means the bridge over the Inn, and it is there that the merchants coming up from Italy passed on their way into Germany during the Middle Ages. This town is surrounded by high snow-covered mountains which you see towering overhead as you look up the picturesque old streets. One is called Frau Hitt, and when it is covered with clouds they say that it will rain, and it generally does.

Innsbruck view from Hungerburg, Austria

King Arthur by Dürer, Hofkirche, Innsbruck, Austria

There are some very fine churches in Innsbruck, but by far the most interesting is the Franziskanerkirche, or Hofkirche, the church with the wonderful life-size bronze statues of the old kings, queens and emperors who were related to the Hapsburg family, and also the monument with the wonderful carved panels of the Emperor Maximilian. We took some lovely excursions while we were at Innsbruck, one to Hungerburg in a funicular railway that goes up almost sheer for over a thousand feet, and you have a lovely view over the city and the Inn valley. Another excursion was to the Stubaital[4] where the view over the great glaciers of the Stubai Mountains and their great masses of snow is very impressive.

---

4   The Stubaital is an alpine valley in Tyrol, Austria. *Tal* means valley in German.

Bronze statues, Hofkirche, Austria

From there we all went to a little town called Mayrhofen in a little valley running out from the Inn valley, called the Zillertal, and there we did some mountain climbing and were probably the first Americans who ever went there. No one in the place spoke anything but German and Americans were entirely unknown, and even the English people were almost unheard of. The valley is very narrow at Mayrhofen and the mountains about are high, many being covered with snow. The highest cannot be seen from Mayrhofen, but you have to go into a little valley for twenty kilometers before you really see it. It is called the Olperer and it looks very white and very dangerous with its great glaciers and snow fields.

GAVRILO PRINCIP

Gavrilo Princip (1894–1918) was nineteen years of age when he assassinated Archduke Franz Ferdinand and his wife in Sarajevo on June 28, 1914. Princip, born in Obljaj in Bosnia and Herzegovina, was a Bosnian Serb nationalist who received training and weapons from a secret society called the Black Hand. He was a slight man, the son of a farmer, who complained that "people took me for a weakling."

Though there is no Zapruder film of the events in Sarajevo on 6/28/14, its horror and its historical consequence are more than a match for what happened in Dallas in 1963. Equipped with a revolver and a cyanide packet, Princip was on Franz Josef Street when the archduke's vehicle slowed to a stop. Princip fired twice from close range, and each shot was fatal. The archduke, dressed in a distinctive helmet with bright green ostrich feathers, was impossible to miss. Princip was armed with a Browning FN M1910 revolver that was capable of firing six .380 ACP rounds.

Princip raised the revolver to his temple to take his own life, but the gun was knocked away. He was unable to swallow his cyanide packet. Immediately identified as the shooter, Princip was beaten by a mob. Police officers rescued him from lynching and he was quickly arrested. At his trial he declared, "I am a Yugoslav nationalist and I believe in the unification of all South Slavs in whatever form of state, and that it be free of Austria."[1]

Wells tell us that "the Archduke and his wife were murdered by an Austrian subject, in Austrian territory." Technically, this is true, as Princip had been born in Bosnia, Sarajevo was in Bosnia, and Austria had annexed Bosnia in 1908. Wells also claims that Serbia had warned Austria of the plot to kill the archduke in advance of June 28. This remains debatable. After the assassination, Serbian ambassadors did claim to have warned Austria; *(con't)*

---

1   My primary source for the details of the assassination and the apprehension of Princip is *The Sleepwalkers* by Christopher Clark, published in 2013.

We then went back to Innsbruck and arrived there on Thursday, July 23rd, and as we were walking about the streets in the rain, we saw a great crowd looking into the newspaper offices and reading the notice of the Austrian ultimatum to Serbia which required an answer within forty-eight hours, and the acceptance of which would have meant that Serbia had abandoned its independence. I immediately thought that there would be a European war as I did not believe that Russia would permit the crushing of Serbia. Serbia could not accept the Austrian demands, which seemed to be entirely unjustified, especially as the Archduke Franz Ferdinand and his wife were murdered by Austrian subjects, in Austrian territory, and moreover the Serbian government had warned the Austrian government that there was a plot to kill the Archduke and advised him not to go to Sarajevo where, as you may remember, he and his wife, the Duchess of Hohenberg, were murdered on the 28th of June. Therefore, I thought the ultimatum was a mere excuse for starting a great European war, and events have proved that I was right.

(con't) they later denied these claims. A vaguely worded telegram sent to the Serbian ambassador to Vienna on June 18 did direct the ambassador to warn his Austrian counterparts of a plot to kill the archduke on Bosnian territory.

Princip was tried and convicted but was not executed due to his youth at the time of the assassination. He died in prison of tuberculosis on April 28, 1918, nearly four years after the assassination.

Archduke Franz Ferdinand and his wife, Sophie, Duchess of Hohenberg

❦

I wished to go right back to Paris where our heavy luggage was, but my family could not believe that war was coming and wanted to keep on the journey as planned. I gave in.

We, therefore, took the train the next day from Innsbruck over the Brenner Pass, which was well known as the greatest highroad between Italy and Germany during the Middle Ages. It is the lowest pass over the main chain of the Alps, and the carriage road was made in 1772 and the railway was finished in 1867. The highest point on the railway is 4495 feet, or almost a mile above sea level. In this pass many battles were fought as its possession was the key to the plains of Italy. You have beautiful views from the train of the snow-capped mountains which tower above on either side. We went down the Brenner Pass from the summit to Franzensfeste, a very strongly fortified town, where we left the train that was going on to Verona in Italy and took a train through the valley called the Pustertal. After leaving the large town of Bruneck you have some beautiful views of the snow mountains; and presently as the train turns and twists up the valley, you have your first sight of the Dolomites.

Louis Vuitton case, Georgina Van Rensselaer

Dolomites, Italy

*T*hese mountains are different from the other mountains of the Alps, and the name comes from a geologist of the name of Dolomieu who first examined the magnesian limestone formation of which they are made. These great rocks rise from the lower tree-covered, or grass-covered, mountains in great columns, or precipices of fissured and curiously shaped rocks, forming innumerable large and small peaks, pinnacles and canons, and the first glimpse of them as they rise like gigantic cathedrals and towers is most impressive and never to be forgotten. Many of the Dolomites are high enough to be, under ordinary conditions, covered with eternal snow and with glaciers on their sides, but they are so steep that little snow will adhere, and some of the highest of the Dolomites consequently have but little or no snow.

Of course, there are exceptions. There is a good deal of snow on Monte Antelao and a great deal on the Marmolada.

DÉODAT DE DOLOMIEU

Déodat de Dolomieu (1750–1801) was a French adventurer, savant, and geologist. The son of the marquis de Dolomieu, he was born in the mountainous Dauphiné region of France.

He made a fateful choice by joining the order of the Knights of Malta at age twelve. When he was eighteen, he killed a fellow member of the Order of St. John in a duel.

As a young man, he journeyed through the Tyrolean Alps in what is now northeastern Italy. There he observed a curious type of rock that bore a resemblance to limestone but did not effervesce in light acid. In 1791, he published a scholarly account of his findings about the rock, which came to be known as dolomite.

Dolomieu at first embraced the principles of the French Revolution in 1789, until the Reign of Terror began killing many of his friends. He then became an ardent supporter of Napoleon.

In 1799, he was one of the savants that accompanied Napoleon on his invasion of Egypt. On the way to Egypt, Napoleon stopped and sacked the Island of Malta, which had been ruled for centuries by the Knights of St. John. Dolomieu was befriended there by Thomas-Alexandre Dumas de la Pailleterie, a French officer and the mixed-race father of the famous author Alexandre Dumas.

Both Dolomieu and Dumas were captured in 1799 by the Knights of Malta and imprisoned in a fortress in Taranto, on the "heel" of Italy. Dolomieu was held in solitary confinement for twenty-one months, in spite of the protests of the international "republic of letters."

While in prison, Dolomieu carved a wooden pen and fashioned ink from lamp smoke. He wrote a treatise titled *Mineralogical Philosophy*, which became a seminal work in geology.

The story of Dolomieu would later inspire Alexandre Dumas when he created the character of Abbé Faria in his novel *The Count of Monte Cristo*. After tunneling through the rocks of the prison at Chateau d'If in an attempt to escape, Abbé Faria wound up in the cell of the wrongfully imprisoned Edmond Dantès. The polymath Faria becomes friend and mentor to Dantès. Faria even writes notes using his own blood for ink. Faria also tells Dantès about a fabulous treasure that is, as Bogart might have put it, "the stuff that dreams are made of." After winning the Battle of Marengo against the Austrians in 1801, Napoleon insisted on the release of Dolomieu as a condition for the peace that followed. Dolomieu died shortly after his release, a broken man.

The region of the Dolomites in Northern Italy is a legacy of Dolomieu.

Dolomites, Italy

We stopped at Toblach for the night and the next day drove to Cortina, on the way passing the Italian frontier and taking lunch on the shores of the beautiful Lake Misurina, which is 1756 meters above the sea level, and from whence there are beautiful views of Monte Cristallo, Sorapis and Antelao and other peaks, but among the most remarkable are the great rocks called the Drei Zinnen, or in Italian, the Tre Cime di Lavaredo, the highest of which is 9850 feet. We drove on after lunch back to Austrian territory and to Cortina. Misurina is 5760 feet above the sea level and Cortina is 4000 feet above the sea level, so that the road descends nearly 1800 feet, and the views of the mountains are very grand, especially as the color of these Dolomites seems to change with

Cortina d'Ampezzo, Italy

the light from gray to brown, and from pink to black.

Cortina, or more correctly Cortina d'Ampezzo,[5] is a large village, much spread out, with many hotels and superbly situated in a broad valley surrounded by the Dolomites, of which you always have the most interesting views. On the northeast rise the Cristallo group with the Pomagagnon and the highest Cristallo peak; on the east the Tre Croci, which we passed coming down from Misurina; on the southeast the Punta Nera, Sorapiss and Antelao; on the south Monte Pelmo, the Becco di Mezzodì and the Croda da Lago, and nearer the Nuvolau and Cinque Torri and the great Tofane, with its several peaks.

⁂

*A*ll these constitute a great field for the expert Alpinist who is fond of rock climbing. Most of them are dangerous and all are impossible for anyone who knows what dizziness is. While in Cortina my son went up some of these rocky peaks with guides and one day I accompanied him to the foot of the rocks on the Nuvolau Mountain. We started from Cortina at five o'clock in the morning, and at nine, after a

5   Site of the 1956 Winter Olympics.

Flatiron Building, New York City. Wells lived just blocks away from the Flatiron Building in 1914.

steady climb we got to the foot of the rocks known as the Cinque Torri. This name means "five towers" because there are five of these rocks; the two largest of which, however, almost touch at the top and it is possible for persons with very steady heads and with a good guide to cross over on top from one to the other. The highest of these rocks rises from the mountain about three times as high as the Flatiron Building and they appear to be fully as steep, in fact, in places they overhang, but by means of the clefts and crags and rough surfaces, it is possible to ascend; but for me waiting below it was dreadful seeing my son and the guide crawling along the edge of the rock with apparently nothing under them, and to see them crossing on the top from one of these rocks to the other. For this rock climbing the ordinary mountain boots with nails are not used, but boots with soles made of layers of wrapped cloth.

———※———

*W*hile we were in Cortina rumors of the coming war became more and more frequent, and I kept getting more and more alarmed and finally I persuaded my family to leave, which we did on Thursday, the 30th of July. Already soldiers were being mobilized, and

Dolomites, Italy

even in the little village of Cortina we constantly heard military bands and bugles and saw soldiers marching away to Toblach to take the train for centers of concentration. We also heard a great deal of rifle practice going on, but, as I say, having decided to leave, we took a carriage over the Dolomitenstrasse, a two days' drive, over three great passes and down again into the valleys. These passes go zigzag up the side of the mountain and down in the same way, and while the roads are as perfect as roads can be, it is slow work going up and exciting coming down. We spent the night at Canazei, almost at the foot of the great snow- and ice-covered Marmolada, the highest peak in the Dolomites, 3309 meters, but which resembles the other Alps and does not suggest a Dolomite peak.

I might say that in Cortina they speak Italian, although the country belongs to Austria, and in some of the neighboring villages they speak German. On the drive towards Bozen,[6] in the earlier stages, you were constantly very near the Italian frontier and consequently the inhabitants generally spoke Italian.

6   Bolzano in Italian, and today.

Dolomites, Italy

In some places, however, they still speak a dialect of Romanche which is a form of the old Latin, but when you get near Bozen you get into a thoroughly German-speaking country.

The country generally is Italian in sentiment and the people nearly all wish that their country belonged to Italy rather than to Austria.

The drive after lunch on the second day from the Karersee to Bozen led through wonderful gorges where precipitous walls of rock rose from the stream on either side for several thousand feet, the road having to cross the stream at frequent intervals and often passing through tunnels bored out of the rock.

Dolomites, Italy

When we got to Bozen late in the afternoon of July 31st, we saw that the people were very much excited about the war. Cannons, camp ovens and other military supplies filled the approaches to the railway, and as we arrived at the hotel, a police official notified our driver that he must leave that night for his regiment and that his horses were required immediately to drag cannon. That night at dinner we heard military bands marching about the town, followed by soldiers, who in turn were followed by all the reservists, who were not yet in uniform, and they in turn by all the young women. All kept marching about the town with halts occasionally to listen to speeches, singing and shouting until four o'clock in the morning.

World War I artillery, La Musée de L'Armée, Paris, France

The next day we decided to leave Bozen early to get nearer to Italy and we took the train at about five o'clock. In each compartment was a printed notice saying that if you opened a window or a door when the train was moving that you were liable to be shot, and at each stop a police official came into each compartment to see that there were no suspicious people traveling and that no men, wanted for military service, were leaving the country.

TRENT AND THE
COUNCIL OF TRENT

Santa Maria Maggiore,
Elia Naurizio

Trent is a cathedral city in northern Italy and the capital of the Trentino region.

Trent is best known for having hosted the Council of Trent in the sixteenth century (1545–1563). The Roman Catholic Church gathered in Trent to plan its response to Martin Luther and the Protestant Reformation. The Counter-Reformation, which began with the Council of Trent, reformed some of the liturgy and practices of the church.

In 1914, Trento (as it is known in Italy) was an Italian-speaking city in Austria-Hungary. The Habsburg eagle was carved into the stone of the cathedral in Trento that Wells visited.

Gianni Caproni (1886–1957), a native of Trentino, was to military aviation what the Wright brothers were to general aviation. Caproni built biplane bombers for the Italian Air Force and other Allied powers in World War I. The United States Navy purchased Caproni bombers to attack the Kaiser's submarine bases in occupied Belgium. Today, a visitor will find the Caproni museum in Trent (*http://www.museocaproni.it/*).

The Trentino region was annexed by Italy through the Treaty of Versailles in 1919. It remains a part of Italy.

Habsburg Eagle, Trent
Cathedral, Italy

Trent Cathedral, Trent, Italy

We got off the train at Trent which is the town where the Great Council of the Church, called the Council of Trent, was opened in 1545. This town is highly fortified as it is at the southern entrance to the Brenner Pass, which I told you about before. It has a beautiful cathedral and other interesting churches, and as we went into the cathedral and the churches we found them all full of women kneeling, praying and crying because their husbands, sons or sweethearts were leaving for the war. It was a very sad sight and one never to be forgotten.

ITALY AND WORLD WAR I

In 1914, Italy, which was sympathetic to Serbia and suspicious of Austrian intentions, was a reluctant ally of the Central Powers. Italy's fears were heightened by the presence of many Italian speakers in the Austro-Hungarian Empire. Many of those whom Wells observed saying farewell to their loved ones in Austrian-controlled Trento in the summer of 1914 must have feared they would eventually serve in a war in which they fought their Italian cousins. On August 2, 1914, Italy formally renounced her alliance with the Central Powers and declared her neutrality.

The Marquis of San Giuliano, the Italian Minister for Foreign Affairs, suggested to a French colleague that Italian debate about the war turned on three issues: morality, advantage, and readiness. The marquis had been the mastermind of the Italian invasion of Ottoman Libya in 1911. The campaign against Libya featured the first use of aircraft as bombers. San Giuliano, described by Wells as being rather "well disposed towards Austria," died in October 1914. To entice Italy to enter the war on the Allied side, the Allies offered Italy a more generous slice of territory (especially Austrian) than the Central Powers could, and the result was the Treaty of London, signed in April 1915. By then, Italian forces were ready.

On May 23, 1915, the Kingdom of Italy declared war on the Austro-Hungarian Empire, their "hereditary enemy," just as Wells had predicted.

The war, mostly fought against Austria-Hungary in the Alps in what is now Northern Italy, would prove incredibly costly for Italy. A visitor to Italy today will find monuments to the dead of World War I in nearly every town throughout the country. Over 600,000 were killed, more than all Americans killed in both World War I and World War II.

Many more were wounded in the war. In 1917, Sergeant Benito Mussolini was wounded by an accidental mortar explosion.

Other Americans would follow in Wells's footsteps, traveling to Italy during the war. Ernest Hemingway volunteered for the Red Cross Ambulance Service, serving in Italy, and was wounded by mortar fire in 1918. His experiences of war and recovery were central to his book *A Farewell to Arms*. Captain Fiorello LaGuardia, the future mayor of New York, helped train American *(con't)*

Train, Cité du Train, Mulhouse, France

We then went on by train to a little place called Mori, and then changed to a narrow gauge railway that was to take us to Riva[7] at the northern and Austrian end of Lake Garda, where we arrived in the early afternoon. On the way we had constantly passed trains full of soldiers and trains with cannon and other military supplies. In the villages we saw trainloads of soldiers leaving and kissing good-bye to their wives and children and very sad they looked, although they tried to keep up their courage by singing patriotic songs. These people were very much to be pitied because they are

---

7   Riva del Garda has been a part of Italy since 1918.

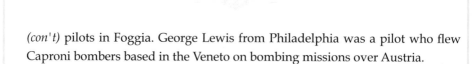

(con't) pilots in Foggia. George Lewis from Philadelphia was a pilot who flew Caproni bombers based in the Veneto on bombing missions over Austria.

At the close of the war, Italy was one of the Big Four Powers, along with Britain, France, and the United States. When the peace treaty was negotiated at Versailles, Italy, despite opposition from the idealistic President Wilson, was awarded the territory that had been agreed to in the Treaty of London. This included the South Tyrol, Trentino, and Trieste. Italian nationalists, however, deplored the absence of Fiume from the settlement and were unsatisfied with their "mutilated victory." Mussolini would exploit this sense of loss and dissatisfaction in his quest for power, which culminated in the 1922 March on Rome.

really Italian and their country should belong to Italy, as I hope it soon will, for they have been oppressed by the Austrians since the country was given to Austria in 1814. None of these people really care anything about the war, or for the matter of that, anything about Austria, except that they mostly hate it.

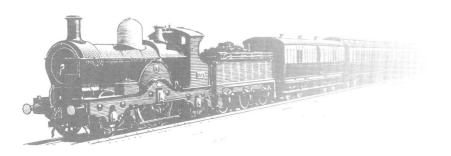

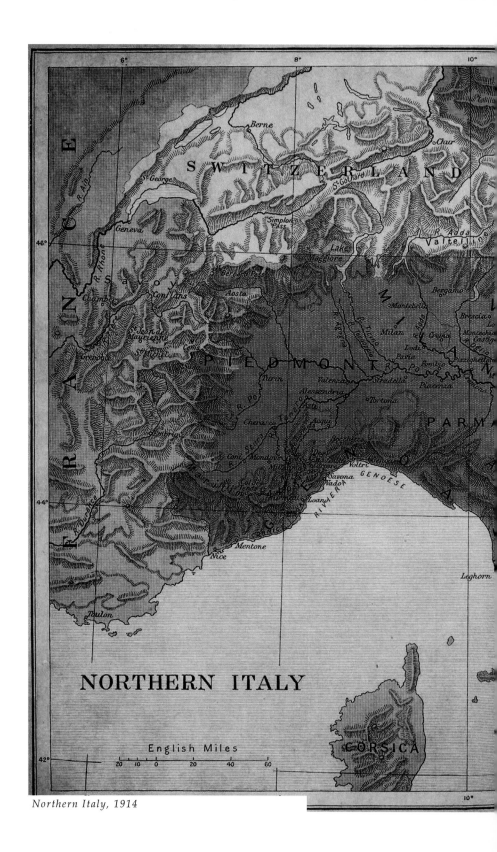

Northern Italy, 1914

View from Lido Palace Hotel, Riva del Garda, Italy

Riva del Garda, circa 1900

Riva is one of the most beautiful places in the world. The mountains at that end of the lake are high and they rise almost sheer out of the lake; and as the lake is very deep, the water has a very blue look such as you never see in water in northern countries; and as the mountains protect the town from the cold winds, tropical plants will grow at Riva as well as they do in Sicily, and you see palm trees and all sorts of plants that grow in the tropics flourishing. We went to the great hotel called the Lido Palace Hotel,[8] which is on the lake and has a beautiful garden running out to a little promontory on the lake, but the hotel had a strange look for although there must have been one hundred, or perhaps two hundred, waiters and servants, there was no one in the hotel except an American couple and ourselves, and it gave you a creepy feeling to see such a big and beautiful place, meant for so many people, so deserted. My wife wanted to spend several days at

---

8   The Lido Palace remains popular in 2016. (See www.lido-palace.it/)

Lido Pa

Riva sul Garda - Giardino dell'Hotel Lido

01110 Proprietà riservata Luigi Farina e C., Riva

Riva. Parco Hotel Lido. Lago di Garda.   737

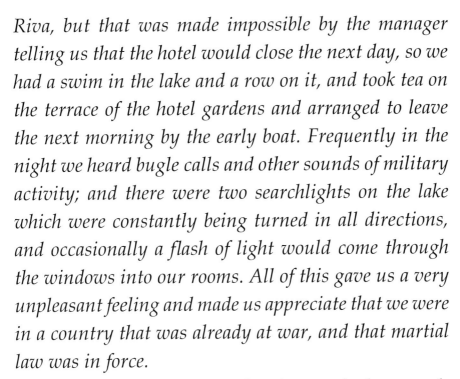

Riva, but that was made impossible by the manager telling us that the hotel would close the next day, so we had a swim in the lake and a row on it, and took tea on the terrace of the hotel gardens and arranged to leave the next morning by the early boat. Frequently in the night we heard bugle calls and other sounds of military activity; and there were two searchlights on the lake which were constantly being turned in all directions, and occasionally a flash of light would come through the windows into our rooms. All of this gave us a very unpleasant feeling and made us appreciate that we were in a country that was already at war, and that martial law was in force.

The next morning, Sunday August 2nd, we made an early start to get the morning boat that takes you to the Italian end of the lake. Most of the lake is Italian, the Austrian part being only the northern tip end, but the Austrian end is by far the most attractive and picturesque. In fact, Riva is one of the loveliest spots I know.

WHY WAS WELLS ARRESTED?

Goethe statue, Torbole, Italy.

In 1786, the writer Johann Wolfgang von Goethe visited Lake Garda and stopped at Torbole near Riva. In his wanderings about the countryside, the great German poet spotted an ancient castle. Struck by its beauty, he began to sketch Scaliger Castle. The dilapidated fortress belonged to the Venetian Republic. As a result, Goethe was briefly arrested by Venetian authorities on suspicion of being an Austrian spy. Nevertheless, he would describe Italy as "the land where the lemon trees bloom."

Something very similar happened to Wells in 1914. He and his family believed they were staying at a picturesque and charming resort at Riva on Lake Garda. And they were.

But there was something about Riva that Wells did not realize. Riva was the center of massive defensive fortifications that had been built, at enormous expense, into the cliffs overlooking the lake. The Austrians were clearly worried about losing their hold on the territory that is now Northern Italy. The Kingdom of Italy, a latecomer to the imperialist party, was in an aggressively expansionist phase. It had opened an outpost in Tientsin, China, in 1900 after the Boxer Rebellion, and fought a war in Tripoli, Libya, in 1911.

The sheer cliffs that descended to the lake were in full view of the rooms at the Lido Palace Hotel, where Wells and his family stayed. These cliffs *(con't)*

*W*e all got into the motor omnibus with all the other guests of the hotel, that is to say, an American young gentleman and his wife (probably bride and groom). The luggage was put on top and we went to the landing quay. As we came near the railway station we saw a train full of soldiers ready to start and the women saying good-bye. When we got to the quay from which the boat sailed, we stopped, and my family got out of the bus and went on board the boat. I stayed behind to see the trunks taken down and put safely on the boat. When the trunks were on the boat, I prepared to follow, but was stopped by a man in a brown and rather dirty civilian suit, with a beard that had not been shaved for several days, who told me that the two

Austrian soldiers in Riva during World War I, Museum of Riva del Garda, Italy

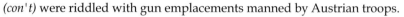

(con't) were riddled with gun emplacements manned by Austrian troops.

In addition to the sensitive setting, there was the timing. The Wells family arrived in Riva on August 1, 1914. Austria-Hungary had declared war on Serbia on July 28. Wells clearly saw and heard signs of the initial Austrian mobilization.

Wells and his family were traveling without passports, which may have also aroused suspicions. On August 5, he would apply for a US passport in Venice, seeking "protection and identification as soon as possible."

Wells's arrest in Riva was a classic case of being in the wrong place at the wrong time.

other Russian spies had been caught, and that now that he had me, all three of us would be shot that afternoon. I protested that not only was I not a Russian spy, but that I was an American. The police official, for such I suppose he was, called up some soldiers with rifles and fixed bayonets and two of them grabbed me, each holding one of my arms, and they made me go to a room nearby which apparently is used for the customs house. There I again protested that I was an American and they asked for my passport. I had no passport and told them so, but showed my letters, my visiting cards, and finally my Letter of Credit to prove that I was an American, none of which, however, convinced the police spy. My son then came back from the boat, he having observed there was some trouble, and I asked him to get me my bag but told him to say nothing to anyone, but simply to fetch the bag. This he did, and I got out of the bag a letter which I had obtained before leaving America from Secretary of State Bryan "directed to the Diplomatic and Consular officers of the United States of America, introducing Mr. T. Tileston Wells." The letter is as follows:

WILLIAM JENNINGS BRYAN

William Jennings Bryan (1860–1925) was a three-time American presidential candidate known for his stirring oratorical abilities. A Nebraska politician with strong rural support, Bryan was born in Illinois. At the 1896 Democratic Convention, he denounced the gold standard, concluding his speech with the exhortation that "you shall not crucify mankind upon a cross of gold." His eloquence helped win the nomination, but he lost this and all subsequent bids for the presidency.

After Woodrow Wilson won the White House in the three-way election of 1912, he appointed his fellow progressive Bryan to serve as Secretary of State. Bryan had been a passionate advocate for peace, declaring, "All the world is in search of peace; every heart that ever beat has sought for peace." During Bryan's tenure at State, however, the Wilson administration did occupy *(con't)*

Department of State,
Washington
June 20, 1914

To the
Diplomatic and Consular Officers
Of the United States of America.

Gentlemen:

At the insistence of the Honorable William F. McCombs,[9] Chairman of the Democratic National Committee, I take pleasure in introducing to you Mr. T. Tileston Wells of New York City, who is about to proceed abroad.

I cordially bespeak for Mr. Wells such courtesies and assistance as you may be able to render, consistently with your official duties.

I am, Gentlemen,
Your obedient servant,
W. J. Bryan

---

9   William McCombs (1876–1921), born in Arkansas, was a New York City lawyer who served as the chairman of the Democratic National Committee from 1912–1916.

(con't) Veracruz, Mexico, and also sent US marines to Haiti. The battleship *Texas*, an American dreadnought, was dispatched to Veracruz in the fall of 1914. Former President Teddy Roosevelt dismissed Bryan as "that human trombone."

After the outbreak of war in 1914, Bryan hoped vainly that the United States might be able to mediate the conflict that raged across the globe. After the RMS *Lusitania* was sunk in May of 1915 with 128 Americans among the dead, Wilson felt compelled to write a strong letter of protest to the German government. Bryan, sensing that Wilson was tilting toward the Allies, resigned in protest and did not serve for the duration of the war.

In 1925, Bryan prosecuted the so-called Scopes Monkey Trial in Dayton, Tennessee, with Clarence Darrow defending. The state of Tennessee had outlawed the teaching of evolution to schoolchildren, and put John Scopes on trial for violating that law. Bryan argued that evolution had not been proven, saw it as undermining religion, and that man was not descended from monkeys. Since Darrow waived his right to make a closing statement, Bryan was robbed of his chance to give his final summation. In the text of his remarks, he wrote,

> Science has made war so hellish that civilization was about to commit suicide; and now we are told that newly discovered instruments of destruction will make the cruelties of the late war seem trivial in comparison with the cruelties of wars that may come in the future. If civilization is to be saved from the wreckage threatened by intelligence not consecrated by love, it must be saved by the moral code of the meek and lowly Nazarene.

Five days after the trial concluded, Bryan died in his sleep.

H. L. Mencken, who covered the trial for the Baltimore Sun, wrote uncharitably that Bryan was "a walking malignancy" and "one of the most tragic asses in American history."

H. L. Mencken

After the police spy had read this letter, he took it to some officers in uniform who were standing a little way off and they read the letter, and as they did so I could see them looking around at me from time to time. After a very short time the police spy came back, handed me back my letter and told me that I could go. He made no excuse or apology, but I was very pleased to go and did so readily. I went on the boat and to the upper deck where my wife and daughter were seated, and sat down opposite to them, but saying nothing at the time, fearing that if I showed any excitement that the police official might change his mind and come back. I can assure you that I counted the seconds until the time to go came and was greatly relieved to see the ropes cast off and the boat start.

A few minutes after leaving we made another landing at Torbole, also in Austrian territory, but after leaving there we soon got into Italian waters, and as the boat was Italian I felt that I was thoroughly out of Austria and was very glad of it.

ESPIONAGE AND WORLD WAR I

Wells was falsely accused by Austrian authorities in Riva of being a Russian spy. There is no evidence that the threatened execution of the "other two" spies referenced in Wells's manuscript ever took place. It was most likely a bluff used in an attempt to make Wells talk. Many World War I spies were, however, executed.

Much of the "surveillance society" in which we live today has its origins in World War I espionage. For example, the British built a sophisticated signals intelligence network designed to monitor German radio traffic during the war. The SIS (Secret Intelligence Service and forerunner to MI6) established monitoring stations from Folkestone to London.

Room 40 was a decryption service of the British Admiralty that would later inspire the codebreakers of Bletchley Park in World War II. Their greatest coup of the war was the interception and decryption of the famous Zimmermann Telegram in 1917. This message, sent by the German minister of foreign affairs to the Mexican government, proposed an alliance with Mexico in the event of America's entry into the war. Its disclosure enraged many Americans, and was one of the catalysts (along with unrestricted submarine warfare and the violation of Belgian neutrality) for the American declaration of war by the United States Congress on April 6, 1917.

Room 40 also decrypted messages that identified Mata Hari, a Dutch courtesan and exotic dancer in Paris who was born Margaretha Geertruida Zelle in Leeuwarden, Netherlands, in 1876, as H-21, a German spy. The information was passed to French intelligence, and the femme fatale was arrested, convicted, and executed by firing squad in 1917. *(con't)*

Mata Hari, Fries Museum,
Leeuwarden, The Netherlands

Mata Hari statue,
Leeuwarden, Netherlands

(con't) In the dawn hours of October 12, 1915, a very different woman, Edith Cavell, was executed in Brussels by a German firing squad. She was an unmarried clergyman's daughter who was working as a Red Cross nurse in occupied Belgium. Her tragic fate aroused great sympathy with the American public. James Beck, another New York lawyer, declared that "the murder of Miss Cavell was one of exceptional brutality and stupidity." Both the Germans and the Allies acknowledged that Cavell aided Allied servicemen in escaping to neutral Holland. Only long after the war ended was it revealed, by military historian M. R. D. Foot, that she had, in fact, been an agent of British intelligence. Her life was commemorated with a statue in London that stands near Trafalgar Square, and a mountain peak in Canada was also named in her honor. The famous French singer, Edith Piaf, was named after her.

The Germans managed to infiltrate a spy of their own into Benedict XV's Vatican. Rudolph Gerlach, a Bavarian, became the Pope's chancellor while betraying Italian military secrets to the Central Powers.

But the greatest German intelligence coup of the war was arguably the smuggling of Lenin from Zurich to Petrograd on board a "sealed train." Indisputably, the Germans helped to finance the start of the Bolshevik Revolution.

W. Somerset Maugham worked for British intelligence in Switzerland, whose neutral staus made it a hotbed of espionage intrigue during World War I. He would later transform his wartime experiences into the Ashenden spy novels.

The popularity of espionage fiction was boosted by the war. John Buchan's *The Thirty-Nine Steps* pits Scotsman Richard Hannay against a nefarious ring of German spies in England in the lead up to World War I. This novel, published in 1915, was filmed by Alfred Hitchcock in 1935 and dramatized on the London stage, to great acclaim.

On May 20, 1917, Major Valentine Fleming of the British Army was killed by artillery on the Western Front. His obituary was written by Winston Churchill. One of his two sons became the assistant to the Director of Naval Intelligence in World War II, but he is better known as Ian Fleming, the creator of James Bond.

Edith Cavell statue, London

AUSTRIA-HUNGARY:
THE RABBIT DUCK

Ludwig Wittgenstein, soldier-philosopher

Ludwig Wittgenstein, who served in the Austro-Hungarian Army in World War I, ranks among the greatest philosophers of the twentieth century. In his seminal work, *Philosophical Investigations*, he discussed the ambiguous ways in which we perceive a rabbit-duck image. Austria-Hungary in 1914 may be the ultimate rabbit-duck in history.

Wittgenstein was himself a rabbit-duck—a soldier-philosopher. During World War I, he was decorated for his service as an artillery spotter on the Russian front. He began writing his Tractatus Logico-Philosophicus when he was a soldier, and completed it when he was a prisoner of war. In it, he explores the relationship between language and reality.

Austria-Hungary was a diverse rabbit, a polyglot empire with at least nine major languages. Over 40 percent of the Austrian Tyrol that Wells visited in 1914 was Italian speaking.

Yet Austria-Hungary was also a unified duck. Franz Joseph had been the emperor of Austria since his accession to the throne in 1848. In fact, the House of Habsburg, which traced its origins back to Charlemagne, had ruled Austria since the fourteenth century. Hungary became part of that empire in 1867. Because Hungary remained autonomous, Austria-Hungary was also known as the Dual Monarchy. In 1914, the octogenarian emperor was a popular figure, *(con't)*

When we left Riva, as we had tickets all the way to Paris and through Milan, we decided that after landing at the south end of the lake at Desenzano, we would go by train to Milan, but as we came down the lake we stopped at the little Italian town of Limone; and there we got that morning's local Italian papers which said that the French army was mobilizing and that Italy had decided to remain neutral in the great war. Therefore, knowing that the French army would require all the French railways for some days, we felt that it would be impossible to go right through to Paris and, therefore, we decided to go to Venice instead to stay until the time was more favorable for going on to Paris. We accordingly had our luggage re-registered for Venice, and when we did so I think the sailor who put the labels on the trunks thought that I was a little out of my head. However, he made the change. We landed and had lunch at Desenzano and then took the train on to Venice, where we arrived at about dinnertime and took a gondola for our hotel with our luggage all on board.

(con't) although his life had been scarred by the suicide of his son Rudolph in 1889 and the assassination of his wife by an anarchist in 1898.

In terms of religion, the Austro-Hungarian rabbit was officially Roman Catholic. The Habsburg dynasty was a bulwark of the Holy Roman Empire. But the Austro-Hungarian duck included large populations of Jews, Orthodox Christians, and even Bosnian Muslims.

Austria-Hungary in 1914 was an empire on the brink of collapse. Many competing minorities were barely held together by an inefficient bureaucratic government.

Austria-Hungary in 1914 was in the midst of a golden age. The Dual Monarchy had a population of more than fifty million, and 80 percent of the population was literate. In 1914, Franz Kafka began writing *The Trial* in Prague. Sigmund Freud was revolutionizing psychology in Vienna. The music of Richard Strauss kept Austrians waltzing. Gustav Mahler's symphonies sent music in new directions, while Gustav Klimt was transforming the art of painting.

Austria-Hungary was a paranoid police state (rabbit) that arrested an American tourist in Riva. Austria-Hungary was a bungling state (duck) that allowed the assassination of its crown prince and might have allowed the Serbian prime minister to pass through its borders undetected in July 1914.

Austria-Hungary was the victim of a secret Serbian conspiracy. Austria-Hungary was the bully that invaded tiny Serbia and precipitated World War I.

Franz Conrad von Hötzendorf, the Chief of the General Staff of the Austro-Hungarian Army and Navy, was the Dual Monarchy's war hawk. From 1906 to 1914, he advised in favor of wars with Serbia, Montenegro, Russia, Romania, and Italy. He advocated war with Serbia no less than twenty-five times during 1913 alone.

Archduke Franz Ferdinand was the duck to Conrad's rabbit. The archduke was an advocate for peace and restraint who opposed Conrad at every turn. He told Conrad, "My policy is a policy of peace. Everyone must learn to live with that." They did for a while. Ferdinand was a reformer who dreamed of creating a "United States of Greater Austria."

And he might have pulled it off had he not made that fateful visit to Sarajevo in June of 1914.

Canals of Venice, Italy

Venice, Italy

I shall not attempt to tell you what a lovely place Venice is and how strange it is to see canals instead of streets, nor that there is not a horse or a cart of any kind in Venice. This story is not meant for a sketch of travel, but merely to tell you what I saw of the war and its consequences.

THE FINANCIAL CRISIS OF 1914

Around the world, one can find monuments to the horrendous human cost of World War I. But one will seek in vain for monuments to the nearly forgotten financial crisis of 1914.

Wells's description of the panic experienced by American tourists and others in Venice was part of a financial meltdown that affected all of Europe.

The assassination of the archduke on June 28 did not immediately roil financial markets. A series of Balkan crises had occurred without triggering a wider European war. The news of the Austrian ultimatum to Serbia on July 23, however, caused the worst one-day drop on the London Stock Exchange since 1870. Bank of England interest rates soared from 3 to 10 percent in a week. Liquidity dried up all over Europe. The London Stock Exchange closed for a week.

Winston Churchill captured the moment in a letter he wrote to his wife Clementine on July 31, 1914. "The city has simply broken into chaos. The world's credit system is virtually suspended. You cannot sell stocks and shares. You cannot borrow. Quite soon it will perhaps not be possible to cash a cheque."[1]

Churchill as First Lord of the Admiralty

---

1   Quoted by David Lough in *No More Champagne: Churchill and His Money*, 2015, Picador.

*T*he next day people had awakened to the fact that there was a great war beginning and that it would be well to get as much money from the banks as possible. My wife and I went to Cook's and succeeded in getting some money there, and then went to the Banca Commerciale, where there was a great crowd, all of whom appeared very nervous and frightened. After a while the manager of the Banca Commerciale came out and informed everyone that letters of credit were of no avail, and in fact that every bank in New York had failed, so that we Americans should not expect to get money from his bank. A great many people began to cry. I am sure that everyone was more or less worried, and we then started for the American Consulate to find out if it were true that the banks had failed and to take steps to get passports.

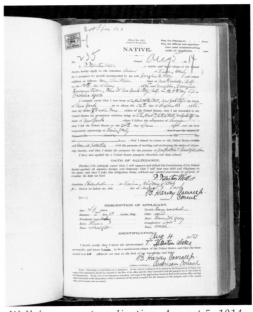

Wells's passport application, August 5, 1914

Streets of Venice, Italy

*T*here were about seven hundred Americans at Venice at this time, many of them in great distress as they had planned their trips and gotten their tickets on lines that the war made impossible. A great many had paid for passages home on the German lines which were not running, or had paid for passages from the North and could not get there, either through Germany or France. Getting back to America from Italy was difficult because in the first place all Americans wanted to get home at once, and in the second place the German steamers were not running at all, and few of the English and French were; and moreover it was feared that Italy might join in the war which would interfere with her ships sailing. Then again there was a great shortage of coal in Italy which made sailing from her ports difficult. Therefore, as I said, there was distress among many Americans and uncertainty among all, because we were unable to find out how bad financial affairs were in this country, and we could not get money in Italy and we did not see how we could get home without money to pay for our passages.

Those of us who had any money felt doubtful if we could get any more, and the rest of us had not

Bridge of Sighs, Venice, Italy

any, so that everyone was very careful about spending money. Under these circumstances none of us took gondolas, but we all used the vaporettos which are little steamboats that go up and down the canals, very much like omnibuses do in other cities, and charge two or three cents according to the distance. Moreover, we all learned that you could walk pretty nearly all over Venice through the little alleys that we had ignored in our gondola days, and we found walking through these narrow alleys exceedingly interesting, and we were able to see the sights in that way fairly well. None of the Americans would go to the Academia, as the great picture gallery is called, except on Sunday when the entrance is free, and on Sunday after church all the Americans in Venice could be seen there.

Very soon after the war broke out the English government chartered a special train to take all the English people in Venice to Genoa and there provided the White Star SS Cretic[10] to take them to England. Nothing of the kind was done for Americans in Italy so far as I have been able to learn, and the appropriation

10   SS *Cretic* sailed from 1902 until 1928, and was used a troopship to bring American soldiers of the American Expeditionary Force to Europe in 1918. She was part of the White Star Line from 1903 to 1923.

Scala Contarini del Bovolo, Venice

that Congress generously made to help Americans abroad was largely squandered in a great junketing party for the benefit of the agents who were sent out to relieve the distress, and who traveled hither and thither, at Uncle Sam's expense.

The hotel keepers at Venice were very good and told us we need not pay our bill to them until we got back to America, and this in spite of the fact that many of them were embarrassed by the effects of the royal decree which exempted banks from paying depositors more than 5 percent of their deposits per month. I suppose that measure was necessary but it worked a good deal of hardship, as you can well imagine.

Food supplies at this time in Venice were, however, abundant and cheap, because a royal decree forbade their export, cutting off the market, and the supply was much greater than the demand. You could get eggs in Venice for less than a cent a piece, and milk and butter and meat including fowls and chickens, as well as vegetables and fruits.

However, there was great suffering in Italy caused by this war. Quantities of Italian laborers have sought work for many years past outside of their own country,

Venice, Italy

not only in America, but in South America, Austria, France and Switzerland. Almost all work stopped in the countries that were at war and the times have been very bad lately in South America, so that thousands of poor Italians had to return to Italy. We saw many of these refugees with their children and babies and bundles. They aroused pity I can assure you. How Italy is going to take care of all these industrious, but unfortunate people, who unwillingly had to come back at this time, I do not know, but perhaps their situation has been improved to a certain extent by taking the places of some of those who were mobilized by the Italian army or navy. When the war started between the great countries who are now fighting, Italy slowly began to mobilize her army and navy, getting them ready for war, and has been slowly but steadily at it ever since.

This brings up the question as to whether Italy is likely to join in the war. It seems to me that she is, because the sentiment in favor of the war and against Austria is growing all the time, and moreover it appears to be for the interest of the country to do so. Austria is the hereditary enemy of Italy, and the people of the north of Italy especially remember too well the persecutions

which they suffered during Austrian occupation not to hate that country, which they do to a man most cordially, so that it never would have been possible for the Italian government to have gone to war with Austria and Germany against France and England, because the people would not have stood it and there would have been a revolution immediately. However, Italy had no need under the terms of the Triple Alliance of joining in the war; her reasons are more than an excuse, as the crushing of Serbia by Austria was contrary to the interests of Italy, and as Italy was not consulted in advance about the note that produced the war, she was not obliged to join in it. If she had been consulted about the note she would have objected to it and then it would not have been sent. It was because the Austrians and Germans knew that Italy would not permit the note to be sent, if she were consulted, that they did not consult her.

However, there is every reason to believe that both Germany and Austria brought every possible pressure to bear, both by threats and offers of reward, such as giving Italy the Trentino, which is the country about Trent and Riva of which I have already told you. However, nothing availed and Italy has up to the present time remained neutral. But the feeling is

CAFFÈ FLORIAN, VENICE, ITALY

Napoleon is often credited with having described St. Mark's Square in Venice as "the drawing room of Europe." The attribution may be apocryphal, but the phrase is just.

Wells, an old St. Marker, must have felt right at home in the heart of Venice.

St. Mark's Square features the Doge's Palace, and St. Mark's Basilica with its four bronze horses, a 323-foot Campanile, and the winged lion of Saint Mark. In 1797, Napoleon carted the bronze horses off to the Louvre when he ended the Venetian Republic. The horses were returned in 1815. When tourists have wearied of seeing the sites, they can repair to Caffè Florian, also on the square.

Caffè Florian *(www.caffeflorian.com/en/)* was founded in 1720, and it quickly became a must-see location on the Grand Tour. Its patrons have included Goethe, Casanova, Lord Byron, Dickens, and Hemingway. Many must have been drawn to the fact that Caffè Florian, ahead of its time, allowed women patrons.

Ernest Hemingway described walking the streets of Venice as being "better than solving crossword puzzles." So after getting lost wandering about Venice, a Bellini cocktail from Caffè Florian (see the recipe in the appendix) may be the perfect restorative. Or you can sip a cappuccino at the world's oldest coffee house and watch the world pass by. Later, when the sun sets over the Venetian lagoon, you can enjoy the evening "battle of the bands" at a table at the magnificent Caffè Florian.

growing in favor of a war against Austria, and I have no doubt that a pretext for the war will soon be found, especially now that the Marquis of San Giuliano, so long the Minister of Foreign Affairs, and rather well disposed to Austria, has resigned from the Cabinet.

At Venice we spent a great deal of time reading the extras of the papers with the so-called latest news of the war, and in the evening we would go to the Piazza of San Marco, and sit down at a table in front of Florian's, order some black coffee which we would slowly sip and discuss the war news and listen to the splendid band.

Caffè Florian, Venice, Italy

Florence, Italy

———⟨⋆⟩———

*W*e had tickets through to Paris by the Simplon and Lausanne and we, therefore, decided to leave Venice and go to Milan with a view of getting through to Paris. We were anxious to do this for two reasons; first, because our luggage, or the greater part of it rather, was in Paris, and in the second place, because we had passages from the north back to America. Therefore, we went to Milan and took steps towards going to Paris by having our passports visaed at the French Consulate and also at the English Consulate as we expected to cross over to England. After doing this, however, we found it practically impossible to get to Paris without undergoing great hardships, and as the Germans seemed to be getting very near to Paris, I did not wish to take my family there, fearing that we might arrive just at the moment of the German approach when there might be a stampede, which would have made it very uncomfortable for us, if not actually dangerous. We, therefore, gave up our passages from the north and took passages from Naples by the White Star S. S. Canopic to sail September 10th, and went to Florence for a few days and then to Rome.

St. Peter's Basilica, Rome, Italy

*W*hile in Rome we happened to be in the piazza in front of St. Peters on the afternoon of Wednesday, September 2nd, and saw the fumata go up black which showed that there had not been an election of a Pope at the Conclave that day. But the next day in the morning we went to the picture gallery of the Vatican, and as we came out and walked toward the piazza, we heard that the fumata was going up, so we ran to a place where we could see and saw the smoke going up white, which meant that a Pope had been elected. Then we stood in front of St. Peters and presently a window was opened on the passageway that runs over the great doors of the façade, and some servants spread out a great velvet sheet with the arms of the late Pope embroidered upon it, and shortly after the Cardinal Camerlengo came to this window and announced that the Cardinal della Chiesa had been elected Pope and had assumed the title of "Benedetto XV." That was on Thursday, the 3rd of September. On Sunday, the 6th of September,

BENEDICT XV

Benedict XV (1854–1922) was the first publicly and vocally antiwar pope to lead the Vatican. Wells was in Rome when Giacomo Paolo Giovanni Battista della Chiesa was elected Pope at the age of fifty-nine in September of 1914, at the outbreak of World War I. His predecessor, Pius X, had died on August 20 as war was spreading across Europe. Benedict denounced the war as "the suicide of civilized Europe." He noted that European nation states were "well-provided with the most awful weapons modern military science has devised, and they strive to destroy one another with refinements of horror. There is no limit to the measure of ruin and of slaughter; day by day the earth is drenched with newly shed blood and is covered with the bodies of the wounded and of the slain."

Benedict's father had initially opposed his entry into the church. Benedict, born in Genoa, earned a law degree from the University of Genoa prior to becoming a priest.

Benedict kept the church strictly neutral in a conflict that found many Roman Catholics serving on both sides of the war. He opposed Italian entry into the war, which took place in the spring of 1915, and also led humanitarian efforts on behalf of POWs, women, and children during and after the war. He supported the brief Christmas peace that took place along the Western Front on Christmas Day 1914, when German and Allied troops played football in no-man's-land. The First World War, and its horrific aftermath, was the central issue of his papacy.

Rudolph Gerlach, a Bavarian priest, became the private chamberlain of Pope Benedict XV. Gerlach, however, proved to be a German agent who paid various Italian newspapers to run articles friendly to the Central Powers. These propaganda efforts were designed to maintain Italian neutrality; they failed in May 1915. The Pope's confidant also used the papal diplomatic pouch to provide intelligence to Berlin. After being dismissed by the Vatican, Gerlach returned to Germany, met with Kaiser Wilhelm II, and abandoned the priesthood.

Benedict was a short man who was nicknamed "il Piccolito" or "the little man." He honored those on all sides of the Great War. He was even commemorated with a statue in Istanbul for his humanitarian concern for the Turks during and after the war.

the new Pope was crowned in the Sistine Chapel. Only three hundred tickets were issued for the Chapel outside of those issued to the diplomatic representatives accredited to the Vatican, to the higher clergy and the Roman nobility. My son had one of these tickets and went to the ceremony. He had to get up at 6 o'clock in the morning and put on his dress suit so as to be on hand for the opening of the service at nine.

Benedict XV, St. Peter's Basilica, Rome, Italy

Length, 615 ft.; Breadth, 65 ft.;
Tonnage, 15,801

R.M.S. Arabic.

SS CANOPIC

The SS *Commonwealth* was built by Harland and Wolff, the Belfast builders of the *Titanic*, and launched in 1900. She was renamed the SS *Canopic* in 1903 and served in the White Star Line. The ship cruised at sixteen knots while diners enjoyed meals featuring baked Cumberland ham and plum pudding with hard sauce.

In September 1914, she transported Wells and his family from Naples to Boston.

In April 1917, shortly after the US declaration of war on Germany, she was converted to a troopship, ferrying the American Expeditionary Force "Over There" to Europe.

In 1925, she was scrapped in Wales.

The next day we left Rome and went to Naples, and sailed from Naples on the afternoon of Thursday, September 10th, for Boston. On the steamer, when it left Naples, were three cardinals — Cardinal Bourne, Archbishop of Westminster, who left us at Gibraltar to take a steamer from there to England, and Cardinals Gibbons and O'Connell.

THREE CARDINALS

Three Cardinals, returning from the conclave that had selected Pope Benedict XV, accompanied Wells on the SS *Canopic* when it left Naples, Italy, on September 10, 1914.

Francis Bourne, born 1861, served as Archbishop of Westminster from 1903 until his death in 1935. Archbishop Bourne, though conservative, wrote, "There is nothing in the encyclical [of Pope Pius IX] which should deter Catholics from becoming members of the British Labour Party."

William Henry O'Connell, born 1859, served as Archbishop of Boston from 1907 until his death in 1944. On October 7, 1914, shortly after his return from Italy, O'Connell presided over the marriage of Joseph Kennedy and Rose Fitzgerald, the parents of John Fitzgerald Kennedy. O'Connell decried Hollywood as "the scandal of the nation," and instructed priests that they could deny communion to women wearing lipstick.

James Gibbons, born 1834, served as Archbishop of Baltimore until his death in 1921. Gibbons lobbied the Papacy for permission for Catholics to become labor union members. He was the author of *The Faith of Our Fathers* (1876), among other books, and three American high schools are named after him. Baltimore's H. L. Mencken, a famous freethinker, eulogized Gibbons as "a man of the highest sagacity, a politician in the best sense, and there is no record that he ever led the Church into a bog or up a blind alley. He had Rome against him often, but he always won in the end, for he was always right."

On Sunday, the 13th of September, we arrived at Almería in Spain, where the ship took on a cargo of 20,000 barrels of grapes packed in little broken pieces of cork. These grapes can be kept in that way, if the barrels are not opened, for an indefinite time and are very excellent to eat.

Almería Cathedral, Spain

Almería Cathedral, Spain

We landed and saw the cathedral and the bullring where they have the bullfights, but unfortunately there was no fight held that Sunday. We also saw what sea power and command of the sea meant, because while we had been able to sail, flying the British flag, as safely as in the times of peace. At Almería we saw a number of German ships tied up to the quays and unable to leave the harbor for fear of being captured by an English cruiser. These ships have to pay port charges during all this time when they are idle, and their crews cannot be discharged, and as they cannot be paid either, there must be a great deal of suffering among them. We were told, in fact, that the crews of these ships were almost starving; that they had sold every loose fitting about the ships in order to get food, could get no more credit and were in desperate straits.

The next day we got to Gibraltar, but were not allowed to land. We saw in the distance in the inner harbor a lot of ships, and were told that they were some fifty German vessels that had been captured by the English and the French.

Cardinal Bourne was allowed to land, and then the captain went ashore to receive final instructions. While

THE NAVAL WAR

Wells, a frequent transatlantic passenger, would have been acutely aware of the naval race between Britain and Germany that preceded the war. Both the British Empire and Imperial Germany were deeply influenced by Alfred Thayer Mahan, a lecturer at the US Naval War College in Newport, Rhode Island, and the author of *The Influence of Sea Power on History, 1660–1783*. Mahan wrote that "the history of Sea Power is largely, though by no means solely, a narrative of contests between nations, of mutual rivalries, of violence frequently culminating in war." Mahan insisted upon the importance of naval power for any nation interested in building and maintaining imperial power.

In 1906, the British Royal Navy launched the battleship *Dreadnought*, which mounted ten big 12-inch guns and was powered by steam engine propulsion. *Dreadnought*'s launch made all other battleships obsolete. Kaiser William II wanted a German high-seas fleet that could challenge Great Britain around the world. Britain sought to maintain the dominance of the Royal Navy in order to preserve its empire, upon which the sun never set. And so a costly arms race was ignited.

In September 1914, Wells and his fellow passengers were certainly concerned about the possibility of attack from marauding German cruisers during their voyage on the SS *Canopic* from Naples to Boston. Wells and many of his contemporaries expected an immediate naval clash of arms between Britain and Germany, but it never really took place. There were some small skirmishes. On September 20, 1914, the same day Wells was leaving Naples aboard the *Canopic*, the German cruiser *Königsberg* sank the Royal Navy's cruiser HMS *Pegasus* off the coast of Zanzibar. Still, no major naval battles took place.

This was against almost all expectations. On August 5, 1914, the New York Times's headlines blared: *ENGLAND DECLARES WAR ON GERMANY; BRITISH SHIP SUNK; FRENCH SHIPS DEFEAT GERMAN, BELGIUM ATTACKED; 17,000,000 MEN ENGAGED IN GREAT WAR OF EIGHT NATIONS; GREAT ENGLISH AND GERMAN NAVIES ABOUT TO GRAPPLE.* The "grappling" did not take place in 1914, though some historians have *(con't)*

we were waiting for the captain to return, we saw a German ship come in which had been captured by the English. It was still flying the German flag, but over the German flag was the white ensign of England. German sailors were still navigating the ship, but there were about a dozen English sailors and marines on board with loaded rifles who told the Germans where to go, and the Germans were bringing their boat into Gibraltar, to be sold as a prize, while the sailors themselves would be kept as prisoners of war. About noon the captain came back to the ship and we started through the straits. As it was very clear we could see the international city of Tétouan[11] on the African coast, and late in the afternoon got a glimpse of Cadiz on the horizon.

The following night we had a dense fog and heard the foghorn of another vessel. Our engine was then stopped and many of the passengers were greatly alarmed, thinking that the other vessel might be a German cruiser. After a while the fog became less thick and we proceeded. In the morning we were astonished to still see land and were told that it was the Portuguese coast, not far from Lisbon, because we had come up in that way so as to be

---

11   A city in Northern Morocco. Its name means *the eyes*.

(con't) argued that Germany might have been able to win the war in the first six weeks if its navy, the Kriegsmarine, had struck boldly from its base in Kiel into the English Channel. This option, however, was deemed too risky.

On May 31–June 1, 1916, German and British battle fleets did eventually "grapple" at the Battle of Jutland—the largest naval engagement of World War I and history's only major dreadnought battle. When the smoke and stench of cordite lifted, the result was tactically indecisive but was considered a strategic victory for the British, as the Germans never did sortie from their ports again for the remainder of the war.

German U-boats did launch attacks on Allied shipping, which proved to be the most important naval conflict of the war. On May 7, 1915, the RMS *Lusitania*, which Wells had voyaged on in the spring of 1909, was sunk off the Irish coast by a single torpedo launched by U-20. About 1,200 people were killed, including at least 128 Americans. The sinking outraged the American public and turned the nation away from neutrality toward sympathy for the Allied cause.

In 1916, Germany moderated its submarine policy by pledging not to attack passenger ships without providing for the safety of their passengers and crew. But on January 31, 1917, Kaiser William II reversed course, ordering the resumption of unrestricted submarine warfare against Allied shipping. This desperate move helped tip the United States Congress, led by President Wilson, into declaring war on Germany on April 6, 1917.

Battleship Texas, *the only dreadnought-class ship still afloat, La Porte, Texas*

under the protection of the British cruisers which were patrolling to protect English shipping. We then struck across to the Azores and arrived at Ponta Delgada on the island of St. Michaels on Thursday, the 17th of September. Here again we saw three German ships tied up in port and not daring to leave.

Our ship was too large to go into the little harbor so we anchored outside and the emigrants, who wished to sail with us, were brought out in small boats towed by a steam launch. As it was very rough they had a good deal of trouble coming up on the ladders on the ship's side, and many of them got wet, but they were all taken on board safely, even the women and the babies, by the skill and attention of our sailors. We also got a lot of pineapples which are very different from the pineapples you get in New York. They are grown under glass and the fruit inside the rind had the color of an orange and is not white like the South American pineapples which we have here. These pineapples are sold in London at Christmastime frequently for a guinea apiece, so you see that they are much higher priced pineapples than the ones we have, but if they are dearer, they are also certainly very much better.

Boston waterfront, Massachusetts

From the Azores we sailed on to Boston and no incident worthy of note occurred. Many people talked of the German cruisers but we were not allowed lights in our staterooms until two days before we got to Boston and saw none. An English cruiser was seen, however, as we came out of Ponta Delgada, and she signaled to us and allowed us to proceed.

We were all exceedingly glad to arrive and to be home again. Especially as the ship had been very crowded and the voyage from Naples to Boston, on account of the stops and the detour to Lisbon, took two weeks.

Epilogue

Wells and his family were inconvenienced by the outbreak of World War I. The war had much graver implications for millions of others. Over sixty-five million men were mobilized to fight in the war. Many of the men whose tearful farewells to wives, sweethearts, and mothers Wells witnessed in Trent Cathedral in 1914 would never return. About one in eight, or over eight million, of those who mobilized were killed in combat. More British, French, and Italians died in World War I than in World War II. Many more were wounded (including both Hitler and Mussolini), and thousands were affected by poison gas. Total deaths caused by World War I, including civilian and noncombat related, amounted to around seventeen million. The Spanish Flu that began in 1918 and was made more lethal by the war, spread in part by soldiers returning home, claimed the lives of another fifty to one hundred million around the globe. Astonishingly, another two were added to the total number killed as a direct result of World War I when, in 2014, two Belgian workmen were killed by a munition from that war.

Tomb of Marshal Foch, Les Invalides, Paris, France

The First World War was the costliest in Western history up to that point (exceeded perhaps only by the Taiping Rebellion in China, which may have cost twenty to thirty million deaths from 1850–1864). It was the original catastrophe of the twentieth century that sowed the seeds for future tragedies. The war shattered the stability of much of the world and destroyed four empires: Austro-Hungarian, German, Ottoman, and Russian. The Bolshevik Revolution in Russia would have bloody consequences for the remainder of the twentieth century. The bitter peace of Versailles would lay the groundwork for World War II. France's Marshal Ferdinand Foch proved to be a modern Cassandra when he declared, "This is not peace. It is an armistice for twenty years."

Pope Benedict XV and William Jennings Bryan described the experience of the war in nearly identical terms: it was the suicide of civilization. Curiously, the American writer H. L. Mencken described Bryan as "the fundamentalist pope."

President Wilson led America into "a war to end all wars" in April 1917. Over one million members of the American Expeditionary Force would serve "over there" before the war ended in November 1918. The League of Nations, championed by Wilson, was formed to avoid the escalation of future conflicts. The US Senate, however, rejected membership in the League of Nations.

Upon his return to America, Thomas Tileston Wells resumed his duties with Lexow, MacKellar & Wells, but his experience in 1914 must have fundamentally changed him. First, he became an amateur historian, writing *An Adventure in 1914* sometime between

Serbian Relief Committee of America poster, World War I

September 1914 and May 1915. Second, he became the chairman of the Serbian Relief Committee of America from 1915–18, helping steer humanitarian aid to that war-torn country. In March of 1915, seed corn, flour, and agricultural tools began flowing from America to the Serbians.

Unlike most of his countrymen in 1914–1915, Wells did not remain neutral. His arrest by Austrian authorities may have affected his attitude toward the Central Powers. He campaigned for Serbian Relief declaring, "The conditions in Serbia have been bad, but they are rapidly getting worse because the people, having been driven from their farms and villages by the Austrian invasion, have been herded into concentration camps where only the barest necessities of food have been available to keep them alive, and where sanitary precautions are impossible. The result has been that typhus fever has now broken out, which is likely to decimate that brave people unless medical help and nourishing food can be rapidly supplied to them."[1]

Wells's efforts helped to save many Serbian lives during the war. Serbian Relief also provided aid to Russia and Romania. Wells's work on behalf of Serbia was part of a larger American philanthropic effort during World War I. Herbert Hoover established his reputation as the Great Humanitarian as chairman of the Commission for Relief in Belgium, which helped feed the Belgian population during the war.

Perhaps as a result of contacts made during the war, Wells, in 1918, became the Romanian consul general to America. He was

---

1   April 1, 1915, *Delaware County Daily Times*

Georgina Van Rensselaer, Wells's daughter

based in New York City, but he returned many times via transatlantic liners and trains to Romania.

An America that was weary of war and foreign entanglements celebrated during the Roaring Twenties. The US mint produced a silver Peace Dollar coin from 1921 to 1935. Anti-German war propaganda contributed to the passage of Prohibition, which struck a blow against German-American brewers.[2] Wells's daughter, Georgina, made bathtub gin during Prohibition.

In 1926, Wells served as chairman of the executive committee of the Society of the Friends of Romania, which coordinated Queen Marie's visit to the United States. The queen's visit was a great success. She toured Niagara Falls, and even dedicated the Maryhill Museum of Art overlooking the Columbia River near Goldendale, Washington, in 1926. The Maryhill Museum maintains a collection of Queen Marie's royal memorabilia (*http://www.maryhillmuseum.org/*).

Wells's daughter Georgina married Cortlandt Schuyler Van Rensselaer of New York. Georgina enjoyed dressing up in Romanian peasant costume. The couple produced two daughters, my mother Nina and my aunt Catherine Van Rensselaer. Wells enjoyed spoiling his granddaughters with cakes and ice cream when they visited him on East Seventy-Sixth Street (today just across from the Carlyle Hotel).

Wells continued to pursue his love of history. In 1931, he self-published a short book titled *The Hugers of South Carolina*, about five

2   See *Last Call: The Rise and Fall of Prohibition*, by Daniel Okrent, 2011.

Wells and his granddaughters, Nina and Catherine Van Rensselaer, Bedford, New York

brothers from a Huguenot family who had served in the American Revolutionary War. Wells received an honorary doctorate of literature from Rutgers University.

Wells also continued to travel. In 1937, at age seventy-two, he returned from his last visit to Queen Marie, sailing from Trieste, Italy, to New York on board the MS *Vulcania*. The queen died in 1938 prior to the outbreak of World War II, and Romania began to ally itself with Adolf Hitler. By 1940 Romania had passed anti-Semitic laws similar to Germany's Nuremberg Laws. An intriguing 1938 document sent by the Romanian Patriarchate to the Ministry for Foreign Affairs stated that the honorary consul in New York—that is, Wells—"defended Jews' interests more than the interests of the Romanian state." Could Wells have assisted Romanian Jews seeking to escape to the United States by providing them with visas? We may never know. It is clear, however, that the population of Romanian Jews was decimated by the Holocaust, from 1940 to 1945.

One can only imagine Wells's dismay when Romania declared war on the United States of America on December 12, 1941, after the Japanese attack on Pearl Harbor. He resigned as the Romanian honorary consul general in 1941.

During World War II, many Americans soldiers would follow in the footsteps of Wells. On July 10, 1943, American troops landed on Sicily. On January 22, 1944, Americans began landing at Anzio. On June 4, 1944, Rome was liberated by the Allies.

The caves around Riva that concealed Austrian fortifications in 1914 would conceal Axis munition factories in World War II. Riva

US Troops in Torbole, Italy
Museum of Riva del Garda, Italy

was also a major hospital location for the Axis in Northern Italy.

Americans would also return to Northern Italy. In the spring of 1945, an amphibious invasion of the northern end of Lake Garda was launched. Amphibious DUKWs, like those used earlier for the D-Day landings at Normandy, were employed on the scenic lake that Wells had admired. The 10th Mountain Division, commanded by Colonel William Darby, landed at Torbole on April 30, 1945, just a few kilometers from Riva on Lake Garda. Colonel Darby was killed by shrapnel from a German eighty-eight. President Truman promoted him posthumously to the rank of brigadier general — the only officer to be so honored in World War II. *Darby's Rangers*, starring James Garner, was filmed in 1958. Today, Camp Darby, near Pisa, is the largest American military base in Italy.

Wells lived to witness Allied victory in World War II, but also the occupation of his beloved Romania by Stalin's Red Army. He died in his home in New York on April 23, 1946. He is buried in New Brunswick, New Jersey; his epitaph reads: **PRO DEO ET PATRIA** (For God and Country).

His son John, who hiked trails in the Alps in *An Adventure in 1914*, became a major in the New York National Guard. He died in 1951. Wells's wife, Georgina, died in 1956.

My grandmother, Georgina Van Rensselaer (née Wells), was eleven years old at the time of the family's 1914 adventure. She would often relate to her grandchildren the story of how her family was trapped in Venice at the outbreak of World War I. Georgina, the last adventurer from 1914, died at her home in New York in 1997.

Darby Monument, Torbole, Italy

THOMAS TILESTON WELLS

SEPTEMBER 12, 1865
APRIL 23, 1946

SON OF

JOHN WELLS

AND

GRACE TILESTON

T. Tileston Wells gravestone, New Brunswick, New Jersey

Acknowledgments

How much do you know about your great-grandparents? When I began this project, I knew very little about Thomas Tileston Wells. And much of what I thought I knew proved to be wrong.

This book could not have been written without the aid and support of my family and many friends who helped put me on the right path. I am indebted, first and foremost, to Thomas Tileston Wells himself, and I regret never having had the chance to meet him. It was my grandmother, Mrs. Georgina Van Rensselaer, who first told me about her adventure in Venice in 1914, when the horses were confiscated by the Italian government and her father could not pay his mounting hotel bill. The manuscript of _An Adventure in 1914_ was generously given to me by my dear aunt Catherine (Mrs. Howard Townsend). Interviews with my aunt and my mother, Nina Van Rensselaer, provided intimate details about my great-grandfather.

Traveling in the footsteps of Wells and his family in the summer of 2015 enriched my understanding of his journey. Carmen Picciani, my guide in Riva del Garda, was particularly helpful about the history of Northern Italy. Daniele Falchi, the manager of the Lido Palace Hotel in Riva, kindly assisted with historic photographs. Matteo Pierattini, my right-hand man in Florence, shared photographs of Venice and the Dolomites. The old Grand Hotel Les Trois Rois, where Wells is likely to have stayed, steered me in the right direction in Basel, Switzerland. The Park Hotel Sonnenhof in Vaduz provided advice on taxes in the Principality of Liechtenstein, and a delicious dinner. The magnificent Cité du Train in Mulhouse, France, the largest railway museum in the world, was a source for insight into the style in which Wells traveled.

This work benefited from the input of readers around the world. My friend and collaborator Stuart Laycock provided much input. Peter Werner and Paul Windels III were kind enough to review my manuscript. Milena Mihajlovic was a source of information about Serbian politics. The Romanian Ministry of Foreign Affairs provided details on Wells's service as honorary consul. Nick Noble and Melissa Anderson of St. Mark's School in Southborough, Massachusetts, dug into the school archive to assist on Wells's career as a St. Marker. Sabrina Sondhi, librarian at the Arthur W. Diamond Law Library of Columbia University, gave me tips on Wells's law school days. Tiffany H. Cabrera, a historian with the US State Department,

helped me to explore Wells's diplomatic career. Christine Kyle, my London tennis buddy, assisted with Italian photographs.

I am also grateful for the assistance of my meticulous editor, Elizabeth Barrett. Our talented graphic designer, Blaine Donnelson, created our cover and website *(www.anadventurein1914.com)*. Travis Baechler did a superb job on the book layout and map designs. Vincent Driano, my brother-in-law and business manager, was always invaluable and encouraging.

Finally, this book would not have been possible without the patience and understanding of my dear wife, Maria Driano. *Grazie, amore!*

Suggested Reading

Alvarez, David. *Spies in the Vatican: Espionage & Intrigue from Napoleon to the Holocaust*. Lawrence, KS: University of Kansas Press, 2002.

Beck, James M. *The Evidence in the Case*. New York: Grosset & Dunlap, 1915.

Beck, James M. *The War and Humanity*. New York: G. P. Putnam's Sons, 1916.

Clark, Christopher. *The Sleepwalkers: How Europe Went to War in 1914*. London: Penguin Books, 2012.

Ferguson, Niall. *The Pity of War: Explaining World War I*. New York: Basic Books, 1999.

Goebel, Julius. *A History of the School of Law, Columbia University*. New York: Columbia University Press, 1955.

Hastings, Max. *Catastrophe 1914: Europe Goes to War*. New York: Knopf, 2013.

Hemingway, Ernest. *A Farewell to Arms*. London: Jonathan Cape Ltd, 1929.

Langley, Lester D. *The Banana Wars: United States Intervention in the Caribbean, 1898-1934*. Wilmington, DE: SR Books, 2002.

Lewis, Edward Davis. *Dear Bert: An American Pilot Flying in World War I Italy*. Florence, Italy: LoGisma, 2002.

Lough, David. *No More Champagne: Churchill and His Money*. New York: Picador, 2015.

MacMillan, Margaret. *The War That Ended Peace: The Road to 1914*. New York: Random House, 2013.

McMeekin, Sean. *July 1914: Countdown to War*. London: Icon Books, 2013.

Nietzsche, Friedrich. *Ecce Homo: How One Becomes What One Is*. London: Penguin Books, 2005.

Okrent, Daniel, *Last Call: The Rise and Fall of Prohibition*. New York: Simon & Schuster, 2010.

Rankin, Nicholas. *Churchill's Wizards: The British Genius for Deception 1914-1945*. London: Faber and Faber Ltd, 2008.

Rose, Lisle A. *Power at Sea: The Age of Navalism*, 1890-1918. Columbia, MO: University of Missouri Press, 2007.

Stone, Norman. *World War One: A Short History*. London: Penguin Books, 2007.

Tuchman, Barbara W. *The Guns of August*. New York: Macmillan Publishers, 1962.

Witt, John Fabian. *Lincoln's Code: The Laws of War in American History*. New York: Free Press, 2012.

Wittgenstein, Ludwig. *Philosophical Investigations*. Oxford Blackwell, 2001 (first published 1953).

Wittgenstein, Ludwig. *Tractatus Logico-Philosophicus*. New York: Harcourt, Brace and Company, 1922.

Photo & Illustration Credits

All other photos by Christopher Kelly

An Adventure in

1914

Recipes

Bellini Cocktail

I) **Bellini Cocktail**

This was invented in Harry's Bar in Venice in 1934. The key to a perfect Bellini is the use of fresh seasonal peaches. A splendid summer drink!

> *Ingredients:*
> > *2 white peaches, peeled and puréed*
> > *1 bottle of chilled prosecco*
> > *4 chilled champagne flutes*
> *Directions:*
> > *Fill the glasses 1/3 full with peach purée*
> > *Add prosecco to top and stir*
> *Serves four*

Café Liégeois

II)   Café Liégeois

The keys to this dessert are freshly made whipped cream and good coffee.

Ingredients:

1 ¼ cup espresso or strong coffee

2 cups whipping cream

2 tablespoons powdered sugar

1 teaspoon vanilla extract

2 cups of vanilla or coffee ice cream

Cocoa powder

Directions:

1. Make the espresso in advance. Cool for a few minutes and then refrigerate for at least 1 hour.

2. Put 6 dessert glasses in the freezer for approximately 30 minutes.

3. Whip the cream in a cold bowl until peaks start to form. Add the powdered sugar and vanilla extract, and continue whipping until the cream is firm.

4. Divide the coffee among the six glasses. Add the ice cream and top with whipped cream.

5. Dust with cocoa powder

Serves six